Worrier to Warrior

Intuitive Healing Tools for Powerful Women

By **Maria Davis**

Maria Davis, Founder and CEO of Maria Heals is a Medical Intuitive, Speaker, and Spiritual Business Mentor who supports business owners, leaders, and healers manifesting bigger and better businesses, relationships, and opportunities. Maria has helped hundreds of business owners over the past 20 years to grow and expand their business in different parts of the world with ease and grace.

Maria runs Circles and 1-on-1 coaching programs helping successful leaders, healers, and entrepreneurs develop deeper spiritual growth and energy mastery. Her focus in her own words: "My dedication is to be inspired and to inspire".

www.mariaheals.com

Photographs of Maria by Francine Schaepper
Cover design, editing, and additional images by Paula Acuña
Book design by Ana Ximena Santibañez

To my husband, Mark, who is the love of my life and my biggest supporter.

To my children, Gabrielle and Robert who are my biggest inspirations and teachers. The light in you is the source of courage, power and wisdom.

Prologue

As we evolve and get to know ourselves deeper, we start a constant journey of discovery. We associate success and growth with "doing things better" or "doing things right". Usually our process is connected with this two very definite questions: ***What is wrong with me? How can I fix it?***

In the following pages you will find why stepping out of these questions and really going into a gentle, kind, smooth and honest process will be the difference between living as a Worrier and turning into a Warrior.

What can give you strength, health, and balance? What elements have you neglected in your life that could allow you to feel like the powerful and whole human being that you truly are?

In this book, Maria will share with you an honest, experienced, and powerful set of lessons that will allow you to reconnect with your place in nature, as a powerful life-force. There are no quick and easy formulas, but there is a fun and exciting journey of discovery. Maria's knowledge will allow you to experience your growth first-hand, finding proof around you and within you of the magic that makes us human. Enjoy the ride!

-Ana Ximena Santibañez
Strategist & Business Consultant

Introduction

After my near-death experience in 2019, my soul's mission was clear.

Every day I live to fulfil this mission. As I returned from my near-death experience, I was given a few messages and began a new journey.

"You are to write a book.
The title is Worrier to Warrior.
Your mission is to dial down fear and dial up intuition."

The message came to me loud and clear.

The other message I got was that we are never alone. To hold someone's hand and feel the support is a gift and a healing in itself.

As you read this book, I wish for you that your gifts of healing are revealed at a deeper level.

May you open your heart to heal the stories held in your cells so you fulfil your soul's mission too.

With gratitude, I thank you for making the journey from Worrier to Warrior.

Part 1 - The Worrier

Chapter 1 - What is healing?

*F*or the longest time, I thought that healing was something others do for us. Something we looked for outside of ourselves, and then another person did *to* us.

And then, I became a healer. I started to ask myself: can something called "healing" exist in and on itself? I knew that when people came to me for healing, they left feeling lighter. So, was that healing? A change? Yes, it was. It was a shift in energy.

Healing is nuanced. Healing happens, not from someone else, but from your intention. As soon as you decide to heal, you need support to access that internal mechanism that is going to help you heal. So, does that turn you into a healer? Yes, and no. Everyone has healing capacity. You heal others when you share kindness, softness, or when you hold someone's hand. The support, care, and kind words you give to others is a kind of healing. All those are small healing actions anyone can do. The Soul wants connection, our spirit, our very human essence, is all about connection.

Healing is the transference of energy from one person to another. It took me a long time to appreciate that. The healing frequency exists, even if you can't see it. But you can surely feel it. I believe healing is a mix of intention and opening your heart to receive. Opening yourself to something different from what you already know, and then recalibrate your energy system to a new version of yourself. To me, that is healing. I can teach you all the processes to support you on that journey, but at the end of the day, it's all up to you. You have to do them, you need to activate this energy in you.

There's this thing called the mirror effect. It's the principle behind my Coaching Circles. When people support each other to achieve something, they access an interpersonal energy web that propels them in a very unique way. Have you ever felt exhausted just by walking into a room full of people? That happens because your energy system is somewhat porous, too open to the influence of others, and the energy either filters through you or gets attached to your system. You feel drained, sad, or overwhelmed. You may even experience despair because it triggers other wounds. That same principle can be reversed, when you join a circle or facilitation process.

As people come together to support each other, there's an energy transfer between humans, going through our nervous system, recalibrating everyone. Then you feel lighter. That is the easiest way to heal, having other nervous systems help you recalibrate through collaboration. We calibrate and collaborate with the forces we can't see, inside an energy matrix that is available to us all.

When such collaboration happens, any resistances you have will dial down as you can see you're not alone. As you realise others experience the same, or similar challenges, you get a sense of belonging, and after that comes a sense of commitment. A commitment to explore more. Once you experience a little bit of healing, you open access to your own healing abilities. Once you experience a small change you start building belief. You embody the truth that healing is possible for you, and then you're on the path to explore more and more.

Healing as an individual and collective process.

You could then consider that healing is a collective process. This is only partially true. Healing starts with the "I". Once you say "I need healing" you've set an intention. You are moving energy already. I know for sure, as soon as people book a session with me, their healing has started. They've decided they need support. Their intention is clear: "I'm going to heal this, I need support." I don't need to do anything at this point. Other healers don't need to do anything. The intention is powerful in and of itself. It's been said, heard, seen, and witnessed.

When I interact as a healer, I then provide the tools. I have several that I apply with clients. For example, we can do a shamanic process, use breath work, do embodiment, or wound clearing techniques. I sometimes do an elevating of the shadows for the client, so that light comes through. I have countless processes to support them with their healing, returning them to homeostasis, which is balance and alignment. Ultimately, it's their open heart that will allow them to receive and feel that they deserve to feel better. From this space, the body, mind, and soul know what to do to heal. A new rhythm is adopted. A new way of being.

When it comes to collective healing, there are nuances. For example, religions are great when it comes to collective prayer. When someone says: "please send me prayers" the collective can heal in a powerful way. It works. We put all our energies together, stirring them up, making what needs to be healed fall away or transmute. Light shines over this person through the collective. There's power behind people coming together with the same intention. It's been proven through activism, social change, and other cultural aspects.

Other societal narratives may have the same effect but in a different direction; oppression, fear, or other beliefs, that limit us and prevent us from healing. Same energy, and power, used for opposing purposes.

That is why the 12-step process originated from Alcoholics Anonymous works so well. We all start with the one and then connect to the collective. As you do so, you're plugging into a bigger source than yourself. This source includes a lot of people with a similar intention or an energy you want to tap into.

There's, of course, a challenge to group energies. With lots of people, comes lots of different energy with personal projections. This is not uncommon in the state of the process to take on other people's stuff, or to project ourselves onto them. Unwanted stuff we all carry with ourselves will always be there, and we must learn to deal with it. It can get really heavy. But still, being on that same boat, knowing that we can count on each other, lightens the load.

Being heard and witnessed is a crucial step towards healing.

When an individual heals, the collective is healing as well. Every individual that chooses to heal and succeeds in doing so, is making a contribution. Even if that means just knowing you are worthy, you deserve to have dreams and desires and accomplish them. Knowing you can be whatever you aspire to be, without all the narratives that hold you back. Show the world healing is possible. Not just physical healing, but also mental, emotional, and spiritual. Then, as you become a leader, you stand in your power and can contribute so much more.

Damaging social narratives that stall your healing process.

As I explained before, collective narratives are powerful energies that can affect our path to healing. But there's one that has become very popular and widely spread in our modern culture.

"You're not enough."

You don't have enough, you're not enough. You don't have enough skills, you don't have enough money, you don't have enough love, you don't have what it takes.

Belonging is so important for us as a human species! We need to belong to a community to feel safe. It's a very basic and powerful survival instinct. But if you're feeling that you're not enough, you're not going to belong fully and therefore will always feel afraid on a subconscious level.

Belonging means being fully accepted by others, including all of your stuff: the shadow, the light,   all. It means not hiding any parts of you. Belonging requires a commitment to really know yourself fully. To be able to connect, commit and contribute. When you belong fully to yourself, you can then commit to yourself and others. It's a cycle that starts within you. Know yourself, so you can understand and own your worth.

As of this writing, immunity is a big thing within the collective. I'm an anatomist. I've studied immunology and how the immune system works. Also, as a psychic, I've actually seen the way it works energetically. As a Medical Intuitive and as a Spiritual Mentor, I work with my clients to access their strength and courage to be who they want to be, to take action. The immune system is interactive with our emotional body and our mental body, it builds pathways to a new you. It's all about flow. The immune system is plasma in flow. Auto-immune diseases, also prevalent in our western society, are a version of the body eating itself.

It's hard to tell when your immune system isn't working properly. Auto-immune disorders are usually hard to diagnose. The individual will experience overwhelming fatigue, chronic fatigue syndrome, fibromyalgia, even some forms of multiple sclerosis. A lot of people walk away in despair, not knowing what to do about the way they feel. We are not taught how to process emotions. It is a skill that is missing but one which is so important when navigating the path to wellness, joy and balance.

The negative emotions behind diseases related to the immune system are guilt and shame. Once you experience those emotions you move to feel alone and in despair. Then addictions may come, as a way to unplug and feel better. So, if the health of our immune system is related to our emotions, and many of our social narratives are often linked to guilt and shame, don't you find it interesting that we suddenly face a worldwide disease affecting our immune system?

I believe there's an energy shift, a healing process happening in the world right now. Some of these experiences are a catalyst to raise our awareness and move to reclaim part of who we really are. Owning and processing our emotions is also part of this process.

Most people have difficulties articulating how they feel. There's a disconnect between their language and their emotions, there's a lack of a cognitive connection, a framework that is missing. The energy gets stuck in your system if you're not able to express your emotions. Imagine repressing what you feel for years and years, building layer over layer that needs to be released. Being able to fully feel your emotions, and to process them, is an important part of healing. But first and foremost comes the motivation, the intention. Recognising where you are and deciding where you want to go.

My journey as a Medical Intuitive.

A Medical Intuitive to me is someone who can see inside the body and access information that other people can't. Some

Medical Intuitives say that they can scan the different layers of the body like an x-ray machine. My background is a little different, so my gift manifests in a different way.

I studied and was a teacher of Anatomy and Physiology, I knew how the body should function in homeostasis. When someone had an energy disturbance, I would know it. I'm very empathic, very sensitive, although I wasn't always aware that this was an intuitive gift. I had no language around it. I did not know that it was a thing. It was so natural to me. It was innate but did need development on how to share it with those I am here to support to heal. I started noticing during my training that I instinctively knew any function missing in a person's system, or muscles that weren't properly working. During my practice as a massage therapist, I felt what was wrong with my clients before they came to me. The healing process for them became more than just physical therapy, emotional, mental, and spiritual healing followed as a natural part of the process. I discovered I was able to tap into all levels, I could see disturbances and misalignments in their energetic system.

I now tap into my medical intuition consciously. Information starts coming as soon as I start reading the form that my clients fill up as part of the onboarding process. Sometimes, just by tapping into their name, I can sense what's happening to them. Then I'll read all their information and I can sense their energy and core wound. I'll then work through the energy systems.

When people first come for medical intuition advice, they are in fear. They come with the "please-fix-me" mindset. They want to know what's happening to them, how they are "broken". They want more information and instructions as to what needs to be done next. They want a series of steps. When they work with me long-term they discover that healing is an evolution process, not a "fix-what's-broken" one. They start to empower themselves. They ask themselves the question: *Can I create a better life for myself?* Then they finally discover they are their own healers.

From intuition to energy mastery.

Energy mastery is a prerequisite for success. Success can be considered as healing yourself, creating the life you want, or growing the business of your dreams. If you don't know your energy system, the way you uniquely process energy, and the flow of energy inside of you, then you're going to have more constant disruptions. Especially if you decide to create a life around a business where you are the brand. You will have to know what your leadership style is, what your energy container is, what your agency is, and how you can expand both your capacity and your agency as a leader in the world. If you don't know that, you won't evolve, and therefore you won't grow, and neither will your business. I know this from personal experience.

As my own business evolved, I would hire business coaches that had a strategy, but didn't take into account my wounds or my energy. Not to mention how sensitive I was to the environment, or the distractions that would be unconscious to me, but that were really impactful on me. Having someone who can mentor you to access unconscious biases, which is totally normal is, a gift for you and your soul's mission. This is how I discovered the importance of intuition and energy in business. Because I wanted someone like me in my corner, I decided to help women evolve themselves and their business energetically, healing, removing blocks, empowering themselves. That is the work I do inside my circles.

Inside the circles we ask questions that create awareness and work through them. What is disturbing your energy? Do you want to keep it or release it? Is it a motivator that inspires you? Or on the contrary, does it bring you down? Is this disturbance really a block? I don't like the word "block" but is what people normally refer to as something that is offering you resistance, and the fear behind this resistance. We excavate until you are the leader you want to see in the world.

The "fix-me-mindset" in business leaders and coaches.

So, just as it happens with physical healing, the first approach people will have to make their business thrive is "fix-me". Tell me the next steps. Show me the recipe for success so I can replicate it and get what I want.

It's ok to have formulas and systems. Sometimes you can build them and walk away, hide behind them. But if you are the brand of the business, just like I am, this brand has a vibrancy. You have a vibrancy. You can be an effective leader and create a huge impact on the world. You need to build the capacity to embrace and hold that energy.

For example, my goal is to affect and support the transformation of a million people. I'm halfway there, but if I want to grow the number of people I impact, I need to grow my capacity to hold them and my vision. From being the person that holds half a million people to becoming one that holds a million means lots of layers to remove, a lot of work to get done. But once I lean into all the things at my disposal to work on that process, I realise I can evolve to that and more. As you go through this process yourself, you become a different person, a different leader, and create a bigger impact.

Your business as an energy entity.

Your business has an energetic body of its own. It has an aura, limiting beliefs, and an energetic system. In the beginning, it's attached to your own. As the company grows, and more people are added to the team, it brings in the energy of all people involved. Often referred to as "corporate culture". That is why doing a mission statement, a vision, and values for your business is so important, and why these should be aligned to your own personal values. Even with other people involved, your energy as a leader will always permeate the whole energy system of the company. This provides a referral e framework -a term of reference for when things get wobbly or resistance to growth rears its head.

Then comes decision-making and our ability to manage that energy. We make over a thousand decisions a day, from what tasks to prioritise, the timing of your next appointment, to your overall goals and strategies. None of that is lost on an energetic level. But if we're not aware of this, and we divorce our decision-making process from our energetic flow, we create misalignment. The process from chaos to calm is unique for all of us. It is multi-layered. Creating awareness of your process is a gift for you and the world around you. It's your unique energetic platform. From here, you grow exponentially.

That is why Energy Mastery always comes first, in both life and business. Align yourself to your energetic platform, and then you decide. Take some time to integrate those decisions, giving yourself some space, acknowledging what you need as a person, so that your business not only survives but thrives.

That is the catalyst for growth. For changing from being a worrier to becoming a true energy warrior. Are you ready? Let's take the first step.

Chapter 2 - Overcoming The Worrier Mindset

The healing journey: from "fix-me" to "I am whole".

I'm aware I joke a lot about this, but it's true. *"Fix me! Fix me! Fix me!"* is what I hear most of the time. The first approach we have towards healing is looking for something or someone outside of us to do our job. It's so much easier to have someone else to do the changes we believe we can't do on our own! The worrier mindset is the "fix-me" mindset.

Yes, healing takes some work, but it can be spontaneous too.

Decision-making is an important part of this process, but even before that, there are some layers to explore. First is your ability to believe in yourself. Believing that you can bring change, that you have the energy to take inspired action. Believing that healing is real, that it can happen for you. There is a mental construct in our society, built by certain economic interests, that wants us to believe that we're always sick and that we   always   depend on something external, like a drug or a pill, to stay healthy. The belief that there's always something that needs fixing in you.

Healing, meaning physical, mental, emotional, or spiritual, is a personal journey. You need to explore your unique path. Every soul requires a matrix of different points of access that bring a whole together in harmony.

For example, soul retrieval is a part of the shamanic healing process. The soul has different parts that disassociate from the body. This is called soul fragmentation. As the soul brings together all its fragments it gains strength, but you may not want all parts back. Some may be disassociated for a reason. In order to be at peace with it, and leave that reason behind, you create awareness, consciously decide the parts you want back, and bring them to you. This process looks different for each person since each soul has a different journey.

Pain and discomfort are usually signs of energetic disfunction. The first step is opening the space for the body to heal. Most of us start with a physical approach to pain, seeing physical therapists, or massage therapists, which is good. I did all that myself. But ultimately, we need to understand that there's an energetic component to healing.

The first sign of discomfort usually comes from the body, and the first step we take is trying to take away the discomfort. When people feel the first signs of discomfort, they look for evidence, for a path. They look for stories in other humans that have had similar symptoms that they're experiencing. They sometimes ignore their discomfort, not being sure "it's really a thing" or believing "it'll soon pass" up until they can't take it anymore. Sometimes they even get used to discomfort, in which case the healing process never happens.

For those who decide to do something about it, those who set the intention to heal, a search begins. They first try to fix it themselves. They search for answers on the Internet, which can be confusing, overwhelming, and even counterproductive. There's loads of information out there and most people don't have the knowledge to understand what applies to them. Still, this part of the process is important as it raises awareness.

What's wrong with me?

Is usually the starting question, and then another one follows: *How can I fix it?* or even: *Who can fix this for me?* Then they seek help. Ask other people for referrals. I get lots of clients from referrals from others I've previously helped heal.

The next step is to try to empower yourself. As you reach your first successes in your healing path, you start gathering evidence that your intention can turn into a reality. You look for ways to keep going, to keep progressing. You try new modalities, such as Reiki, or energy healing, or self-help, and self-empowering tools. You are now responding to an internal source, not just looking for something or someone outside of you to fix things for you. You're still in the gathering-evidence stage, so you discuss in groups what works and what doesn't looking for what's true for you.

As you embrace your power and understand your energetic system, you come to the last stage of the healing process, which is moving from a 3D experience to a 5D experience. We'll go deeper on the subject later in the book, for now, you just need to know that the last stage for the healing process is grounding and empowerment. This is the warrior mindset.

You finally embrace the fact that you are living a human experience, acknowledge it, and come to the understanding that there's nothing wrong with you. *"I'm healed, I'm whole, I'm complete"* it's the prevalent thought. You understand healing as work you need to do, as part of who you are. This doesn't mean you won't experience pain. It doesn't mean you won't wake up with a headache. You still need to look after yourself physically, nurture and nourish yourself, take action.

Every step of the healing journey requires a different action. But when you act from 3D, from limitation and lack, you're acting from fear, and so your results take longer to arrive. It's hard to move out of the "fix-me" mindset. Your energy is contracted, holding on for your life, in survival mode. As you move through the second stage you move to 4D, you start tapping into your responsibility, your power. You build self-reliance. You call back your energy. Then when you reach the final stage, living in 5D, without judgment. Embrace your body, understand it decays, take inspired action, fully embracing the process.

Living as a worrier.

Why do we worry? Why do some people worry more than others? Is it true that worry is a habit? These are common questions I get. Worry is a natural process, especially when we're facing any challenges, not just those related to healing.

The human brain is designed to worry. We fear the unknown. Worry is a kind of fear state. It's not always bad, it can get you going, and even motivate you to take urgent action. But for prolonged states, worry can be paralyzing. It grows as we buy into societal narratives and become smaller, consumed by fear.

Worrying affects the immune system. It clogs up with worry, anxiety, or depression, but it needs to flow freely. Think of the immune system as a layer of water over your bloodstream. If this water becomes stagnant, as a clogged pool, slowly but constantly toxicity will build on top of it.

People who worry all the time (and we all know one or two) end up with toxicity run-in through their system, as opposed to flowing with vibrancy and health. Worry also clogs the fascia in your system. The fascia is where all of our memory is held, a sheath of myelin that covers every cell in our body. It's here our emotional connection is. Then, as it clogs up, issues like arthritis or lower back pain appear.

Worrying makes you tired too, which you've probably noticed already. You cut off your source of energy, so you may feel chronic fatigue. Speaking for myself, when I worry nothing shifts. I used to do it a lot when I was younger, and I used to get stuck. But when I acknowledge the worry, recognise it, see it with curiosity, then I can shift. I ask myself where the worry comes from, what initiated it. I hold space for it believing it came to me for a reason. Then I can get motivated by it and move forward, which makes a total difference.

Our society promotes a state of constant worry. There are societal narratives that keep you in an archetype and life pressure created by external forces. This is where intuition and discernment are very important. As you go through social media and news feeds, do a gut check. What's right for you? What do you want to engage with? What are your core beliefs? Stay aware of what you let into your energy system. All this information is external, it doesn't belong to you.

Another societal narrative is the need for certainty and control. That increases our fear of the unknown. That is why so much work is done on staying present, living in the now. Masters like Eckhart Tolle and many others are teaching us the need to live in the only certainty we have, which is the present moment. People heal the past but then worry about the future. It's great to have plans, but what makes you happy today? What does "happy" feel like to you, in your body? Once again, tap into your body, your discernment. We're all born with natural discernment, we just block it due to the limiting societal narratives widespread across our western society.

Stories of healing.

When I think of my personal healing experience, what first comes to my mind is the time I did a community service announcement as I was diagnosed with cancer. I've done a lot of healings and sent out a lot of healing energy to others, and the moment I announced it, I received thousands of emails and texts. I believe I received the healing I have sent out into the world tenfold. I've been a healer for over ten years. I've been part of lots of healing circles and done a lot of healing work for myself. But being held by others, and being open to receiving healing from others, was a big thing for me. It helped me appreciate the true soul connection we can access in the most profound way. I feel the deepest gratitude for the journey of connection soul to soul.

Healing can come in unexpected ways. Keep the hope, doing your way, seek your own remedy, your own guidance. Keep seeking answers. They're out there. Sometimes answers are locked inside of you, and all you need is that key to open the door.

One of my clients came to me with paralysis on the right side of her face. We worked together intensively for twelve days. We accessed what I call the core. As a medical intuitive, as I tapped into her body I could see what was happening at multiple levels, not just the physical. Almost like an x-ray, but I could see it, feel it, and sense it. I then supported her to create awareness around the stories of her past that created the dysfunction.

Every day I sent her healing through meditation, it comes from my hands, directly from Source. But what I believe made the difference was that old familial pattern she released. A story she carried from childhood that kept her stagnant, static, contracted. She was writing a familial book, a legacy, which she ended up publishing. She did amazing work. And as she released those stories, guess what happened? She healed! The paralysis went away.

Another client of mine had stage-four cancer. It was all over her body. It started in her breast, then moved to her spine and brain. We worked together for almost a year. She now had the tools to continue the healing journey. She collected evidence of what her unique healing requirements are. The work made her confident to continue the healing process. Together we accessed different levels of energy that supported the shrinkage of the disease. The main work we did was around her cells, the ones that were mutating. We spoke to her cells and released the stories that were attached to them. We did some work on cell regeneration.

Every time we met, I would introduce the process, she would go away and do her "homework", and then she'd come back to me. It was almost like a full-time job at that stage, the way she embraced her power to take care of her body.

She was also facing marital issues, and as the process moved forward, all areas of her life improved. As of this writing, she's still working, the cancer is still there, but it's significantly shrinking. The moment we met, doctors had given her just a few weeks to live, and now it's been three years since that day. She is very powerful, she's embracing her journey feeling very energetic.

This process is something that is available to everyone. As you connect to your energy and practice awareness it becomes easier. Now let's talk about how you learn to tap into your intuition for healing.

Chapter 3 - Your Body Speaks

I've asked people many times: where do you feel the pain? Where is it located in your body? Or, how are you feeling? The most common answer I get is "I don't know".

One of the things we do in healing is connecting people to their bodies. As energy intuitives, we connect people's bodies to their energy systems. It's about not judging, but creating awareness. Awareness about what you feel, how it feels and how you feel it. I often go to color, texture, and layers as a tool to help them describe what they feel. When they're able to do that, that is when the door opens to more awareness and healing.

The body challenges you. Your energy system challenges you. When it's got something to change, something to say to you, it'll do it through your cells. Typically, it's the pain you'll feel. It will present discomfort, often created via repressed feelings that develop toxicity in the cells. Also, as we move into who we're supposed to be, or where we're supposed to go, preparing for our soul's mission, we physically change. Our transformation is a physical shift.

Your body uses symbolic language through discomfort, pain, and other sensations. So, for instance, when you have pain in your feet, it's about stepping into your next stage, your next version of yourself. As you resist this change, the muscles become really tight. I sometimes see in my clients who experience this pain, entanglements in the muscle filaments, that create pockets of toxicity. This toxicity needs to be shifted. The problem is, as humans, we don't always know what it means, because we don't know our body's language. Instead, we lean into the challenge.

These little pockets of energy that I see are supporting our shift. They're asking us to stop and listen. That is what pain does, it asks us to take a pause. But we don't. From early infancy, we've been trained to move, move, and keep moving. There is a "push" mentality we are trained to do. Always thinking about the future, never able to stay present. We need to train in presence. There are a lot of teachers on this subject, and it's a practice that implies spiritual evolution.

Learn to acknowledge the little nuances that occur on a moment-by-moment basis in your body. Let's face it, we all argue that we don't have time for that. We ignore our bodies because who has the time to feel bad? So, we push it to be better. But what if we shift our perspective? What if we see this as a sign and an opportunity to tap into the best version of ourselves?

What if we let the moments of struggle, these changes in our body, be the inspiration we need?

Our cells speak to each other.

The fascial system is a solid and liquid component that covers every cell in our body. It allows cells to communicate with each other by sending a series of signals. It's also a system of cellular memory. It works like a neurological and spiritual connection to who you are at this very moment, in this very particular time and place on Earth.

There are many layers to the human body, it is very complex. That is why the study of medicine divides it into specialties. You'll find doctors, specialists, therapists, and surgeons that concentrate on one part of the body. But as they do so, they cannot cater to the whole body. Like the entanglements that show up in one part but originate from another part. The body works as an entire system, as a whole. Eastern health models have a more holistic view of the human body and even go beyond the physical body.

There is something really special with every layer and every pocket of your physical anatomy. It's made of dense matter, and we want to create some lightness. It's when we merge the knowledge from the Eastern (holistic) and Western (specialization) medicine traditions that we can truly evolve in our healing path. We need to understand matter, but we also need to go beyond. We must understand these pockets of pain, this energy in your system, both from our physical and energetic perspective.

The times we are living now are amazing, as we are finally merging our scientific knowledge with our intuition. Quantum physics is now bringing new ways of observing and measuring what happens in our bodies.

How to connect to our bodies.

The way I teach medical intuition is a mix of dissection and wholeness. You observe the quadrants of your body – the four sections with the center being your heart.

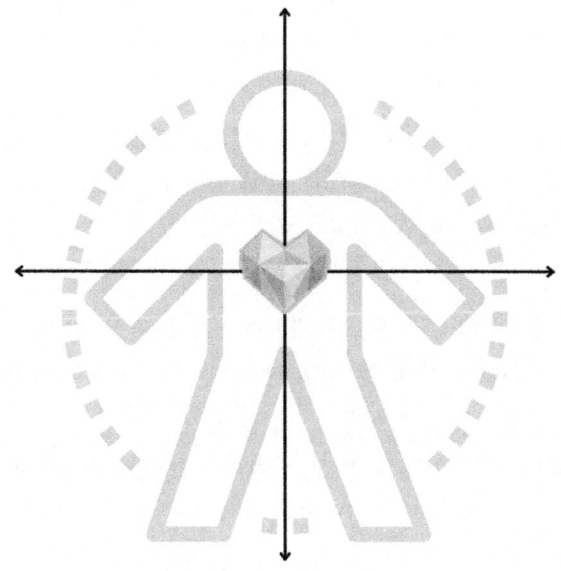

There's above and below the heart, and there's to the left and the right of your heart. These are your body's quadrants. As you assess them, you'll discover the layers.

So for instance, you may experience pain in the foot, and the energetic origin of that pain resides in the neck. Some energetic patterns formed in the body from past-life experiences, and now they need to be released. They show up for a reason, something needs to come to awareness so you can move to the next stage of your journey.

The "hots spots" in your body will come for you to see them. You don't need to understand them at first, you just need to fully feel them. If you overthink what you're feeling, or if you rationalise it and ignore it, then your mind starts playing tricks on you, instead of leaving space for your soul to express what you need and guide you.

As another example, many people experience migraines. Their first impulse is to stop the pain by taking medication for pain relief. This will temporarily ease the discomfort, but it also stops them from going deeper, peeling the layers, and managing the real issue. Pattern interruption with the pause from pain created by medication may feel good. But to go to the core issue, the core cause of the pain is the real gift. The medication can be temporary, but the awareness of the core issue can release the pain forever. I've seen this with clients. It's phenomenal, extraordinary, and inspiring. To connect to the spirit and soul via the physical is a miracle ready to be revealed.

Pain is debilitating and distracting, so yes, let's first manage the pain, regulate it. Once your body reaches homeostasis, you study your energy systems. Explore new modalities to heal and change the patterns for the way you've been dealing with pain up to this point.

In shamanic medicine, the primordial belief is you need to call your soul home. The soul splits into fragments, creating a void that produces pain. The vibration in your system then becomes chaotic. It feels like loud drums that you just want to stop. As energy starts flowing melodically, then you feel lighter and better. That is how sound healing can help. The sound vibration will bring your nervous system to a point that it creates harmony within.

Another process to explore, to help you break this pattern, is to listen to music or engage with art that touches your heart. Read a poem, watch a movie, or even stay in your breath, which is your internal music. Your lungs hold the life force of your body, they have unimaginable capacity. They are as big as a tennis court if you spread them out. Breathing is one of the simplest processes to bring your body back to balance and it's free.

In my practice, I help people learn to listen to their bodies with simple tools, such as muscle testing. Or I ask them to close their eyes and ask intuitive questions: what colors do you see? What is that color saying? What part of your body should I pay attention to first? Then we look at the stories attached to that particular part of the body.

Changing patterns.

To break your patterns and heal, all you need to do is change one thing. Interrupt the way you've been doing things, and then give your body time to recalibrate. We all want fast results, but the body doesn't work like that. It takes a long time for the pain to become chronic. Why should the healing be instantaneous?

There are ways to quickly unravel the source of the pain, and then practices to accelerate the healing, but we need to honor the process, recognise the layers it involves, and also have gratitude for the intelligence that brought awareness. Trust that healing happens under perfect timing as long as we stay disciplined and committed.

Our organs perform different functions, but they also operate on particular energy systems and collect wounds over lifetimes. We sometimes fall into patterns that stop us from listening to our intuition and the call from our bodies. We are busy, so we don't like interrupting our lives to look into what may be uncomfortable.

Having cancer was a wake-up call for me. I learned to both listen to my intuition and support myself. When I became fifty, I ignored the health system recommendation to get a bowel cancer screening test. I thought I wasn't "old" so I didn't need it, even when I was getting a nudge that I should get it. I thought I was too busy, didn't have enough time. When I finally did, I discovered I had cancer. Then, as I went within, I found the reason was resentment built up in my bowel. It came from lifetimes over lifetimes of not healing the resentment. "Re-sent-ment" is sending the same thing over and over again until it builds and has nowhere to go. It putrefies, becoming poisonous to the system. It was time to really listen to my thought. Even the tiny subversive whispers that had become part of me. Acknowledging and creating awareness of my deeper soul truth rather than the patterns I had bought into for survival and belonging.

Cancer taught me so much about how I operated and how I hid my deep truth. I have learnt to be more compassionate and not to judge myself or indeed others. When/if I fall into the familiar pattern, my cancer experience reminds me that there is another way. As humans, we know what we know until we know something different.

Cancer is cells in your body going rogue, and then coming together, getting your body out of homeostasis. They are toxicity that becomes malignant, this toxicity can be both physical and energetic. If you don't work on its underlying issues, it will grow and grow until you start to pay attention to those issues. I was lucky I caught my cancer at an early stage because I experienced no symptoms. My body spoke to me in the form of an intuitive nudge that I kept ignoring. I do believe that Spirit gives you as much as you can cope with, doesn't always give you the whole picture. How does your body speak to you? It could be a pain, bleeding, a nudge, a bump, any signal that needs to be addressed. It's ok to interrupt your patterns and take care of yourself.

We often forget to do our spiritual work, meaning we forget to give our bodies some breath. It's not complicated. Simply find a place to relax, let go of your thoughts, and focus on sending life force to any particular part of your body that is bothering you. You bring life force with your breath, so, breathe into that part of your body, breathe into your pain, your discomfort, your fear, your negative thoughts, anything you need to heal. Becoming aware of what your body is telling you is probably the most difficult part, once you have that awareness finding a tool to heal is the easiest part.

One of my clients, who works as a channel medium, called me one night. She was really scared. "Maria, Maria! I'm shaking all over!" She said. So I asked her to rate this tension on a scale from one to ten. Ten being the most uncomfortable, one being fully relaxed. Then I asked her if she could see any color and what it was. Finally, I asked her if she wanted me to send her energy healing. She accepted, and as I looked into her energy stream, I found her aura was porous. She had been doing a lot of her mediumship work, forgetting about her energetic hygiene. One energetic practice was to clear her energy or ask her guides to do so after each session. She became too busy that she forgot to do so. As I looked at her energy field, I could see that there were spirits attached to it. We addressed the issue by calling on Archangel Michael, performing an auric cleanse to about six feet beyond her body, and then closing all remaining gaps. She slept well and woke up feeling even better.

Addictions and cravings.

Another way our body sends signals is through perceived needs and cravings, which sometimes turn into addictions. The need to calm discomfort through an external source. And guess who dealt with addiction? Yes, I did! For me it was food. I worked the twelve-step program with Overeaters Anonymous, so I understand what it's like to overcome an urge your body sends you.

The twelve-step program is steeped in spirituality relying on clearing the path of obstacles. Obstacles that could come from inherited survival narrative or external paradigms that largely remain unconscious but deeply rooted in belonging. The real challenge is to identify the layers that trigger the craving that leads to addiction. It feels like a need, and that need represents a void. We then look for something outside ourselves to fill that void.

Once the void, the feeling of emptiness is consciously accessed, feelings of safety and security are embraced, and the healing can begin. This is not easy. It requires support and help from others. The healing or energetic shift begins when something changes inside of us, opening space along our soul's journey. But we don't know how to fill that space, we fear change, so from our early learnings, for some it's easier to suppress or numb the sensation. We fill this void with something outside of us, being this food, drugs, alcohol, shopping, whatever you can think of.

As humans, we don't have all the information. We see the world from a limited perspective. It is hard to understand our bodies, to listen when there's so much noise out there. We just don't know what advice is good for us, what information will help us. That is why I think developing your intuitive discernment skills is critical part of thriving. Because when we can learn to trust ourselves, and learn to trust the nuances, then you're on your path to healing. Whether it's energy in your body, incoming messages that you might hear from Spirit, some song you hear on the radio, whatever it may be. You can also ask for guidance.

Ask Spirit to give you a message, to come through your dreams.

So, just listen, listen with both ears, listen with your soul and your gut. And ask for help. There are professionals out there that can support you. Wisdom is not created, it is received.

Chapter 4 - Feeling your energy

We all have an energy body, but we live disconnected from it, just as we do with our physical body, and maybe even more. We still have much to learn.

I have thought this for the last six years, and I'm still learning. I started this work ten years ago, and even mystics and healers using ancient techniques never stop learning. So, don't worry about what you don't know. Whatever you know today, whatever comes into your realm of reality, simply build on it. Trust it's exactly what you need to know.

Create awareness. Be curious. For example, at the moment of this writing, I'm doing a thirty-day energy mastery and audit. I'm constantly checking. The moon, the signs, your elements, what's tapping into your energy?

What's happening to you?

It's really simple. Ask yourself, on a scale from one to ten, how are you feeling?

So, right now, I have the need to ground myself. I feel the need to connect to Earth because I had a really busy week. I see it as an opportunity to come into myself. When you do this exercise you are getting information that comes from within, instead of the outside world. What you do with this information is up to you. What's important is that the information comes from inside yourself.

Many people don't know how they feel. They can't articulate it. When I ask myself how I feel, I need to go into my thinking brain, trying to find the right words. The same thing probably happens to you. It's a difficult task. Words are abstract, and feelings are entangled. So, I'd say I feel a little tired. I feel content. I feel connection, I feel connected, and I feel joy. But I'm also feeling that I should move a little faster, and there's a judgment. So, I'm judging myself. This judgment brings anxiety, another feeling. There are lots of feelings that come with each thought, each moment.

If you ask someone how she's feeling, she'll say "good", or any other kind of generic response. Then, ask that someone to articulate that feeling, to name it. That is a process in itself. I think we don't have the vocabulary nor the process to dive deep into what we're feeling. But once we know what we're feeling, we know what to do with those feelings. We are not trained to name, to articulate what we feel. I've seen it with thousands of my clients and students.

Why is it that we have such a hard time identifying our feelings and naming them? Is it because it's scary? Is it because it's uncomfortable? Because we're too busy? I think it's because it's a complex process. It's layered. We experience so many feelings at the same time! We need time and discernment to acknowledge our feelings. It's a skill you develop. Just like intuition, you're born with the knowledge and the sensitivity, but you need to dial it up. It's an evolving process.

Simplifying the process of feeling your energy.

Learning to connect and understand what we feel is a complex, layered process. Nevertheless, we can simplify it so you can start experimenting with it.

Let's start with pain, which is a very loud, clear feeling, but you can apply this to any sensation you experience. When you experience pain, ask yourself: where do I feel it? Where is this sensation located in my body? What sensations are alive in my body at this moment? Am I on alert? Now... Close your eyes. Use your third eye to see the pain, or to listen to it. What are you hearing? What are you seeing? This is a developmental process, the process of connecting within.

Once you've located your pain or sensation, it's time to discover its story. Depending on where you feel it, there's a story attached to it. For example, attached to a location related to the root chakra, you could find a story about safety. You can then keep asking questions related to your security, so you discover what needs attention. You will discover what you need to release or heal. Awareness of that story is like a switch that turns on the light bulb. You turn on the mind-body-soul connection, and that is where miracles happen.

When you turn on this awareness, you'll notice less pain. Since pain is something that accumulates in our bodies, especially chronic pain. It will take some time to release it completely. We spend months, even years, ignoring pain, so it's very likely we need to bring awareness into many complex layers. Autoimmune diseases, heart disease, cancer, and others are cumulative, subtle pain that we ignored. We kept hearing "rest, rest, rest!" But we kept pushing, suppressing the feelings and ignoring them.

Learning to stop time.

When you decide to heal and let go of the worrier mindset, your job is to listen, learn, and evolve. Learning by really connecting. The excuse you give yourself is you don't have the time. But time is a construct I've been playing with for years. We can either slow it down or speed it up. When I feel the need to rush, to keep going non-stop, I take a deep breath. I affirm: "there is plenty of time". At that moment, time slows down. This happens as I go into an equilibrium, a deep trust that I'm supported. There's nothing I need to do. Nothing. Give it a try!

Just breathe, come back to your breath. Some time ago, when I found that I had adrenal fatigue and fibromyalgia, the best promise I gave to my soul was this:

There's plenty of time.
I'm here doing what I need to do,
for the time being.

Most people live with the sensation that they're falling behind. Falling behind what? When we don't have enough time, when we get the feeling we must accelerate, that is when we need to slow down. I know, sounds counterintuitive. Slowing down is the only way to speed up.

The effects of social media on our energy system.

Social media adds a big strain to this false experience of feeling behind. When you're constantly comparing yourself to others, somehow people seem ahead of you always. I've always been aware of the effects of social media on our central nervous system. It makes us come out of ourselves to be something that we're not. Those images we see, those profiles we create, they reflect that. Maybe it's just my journey, but with my clients, we address this issue frequently. If something affects your central nervous system, it'll take you out of alignment.

It's all about going back to our values. When something affects your brain with a dopamine hit, with likes, reach, and approval you get from others, you must be aware you are the one in charge. Yes, you can use social media in your business, to connect, to share. But when it is affecting your energy you must take charge. Decide what you want to do today. How do you want to impact those around you? How is social media impacting you? Take note. Having a marketing strategy with social media is a start. What would you like to achieve with it?

And I think a lot of spiritual entrepreneurs are leaving some social media platforms because they realised it's negatively impacting their energy. But I'm staying because I'm aware I can take charge. I can work with it. So, just be curious. How is social media affecting you?

It's clear social media plays with human addictions like recognition and social approval. But you can still use the tool with awareness. You can use social media intentionally, to **Connect, Commit, and Contribute.** This is the **Three C's process**, which we'll address later in the book.

For now, just ask yourself if your constant use of social media comes from addiction or commitment to contribute. Are you looking for recognition or are you looking to serve? If you decide to use social media to contribute, ask yourself, how can I be of service to myself and others? How does that impact the collective?

Base chakras and their messages.

The lower chakras are related to our material and physical needs, they are more connected to our human experience. The first chakra, the grounding chakra, relates to security. It relates to how we move in the world, how we live and interact with it. All issues related to money as a stable income, survival, and support from your tribe will show up in this area and the body parts related to them. So, for example, a sprained ankle can relate to your ability to stand, to be here and now. Are you feeling stable and secure?

The second chakra is related to identity. To who we are. That is where we create, where we feel safe, where we get angry. The sacral chakra nudges our devotion to self, to creation, and reflection of who we are in this world. It offers us enquiry into balance, responsiveness, and foundational support. It is a balance of left and right energies, the feminine, and masculine. Often, when we are not balanced energetically, we will see it in our posture. In every human body I have worked with, there is a stronger side. This is telling of where we are in the world. We thrive when we feel balanced. This is the role of the sacral chakra to balance our primordial needs with our soul mission. We ask ourselves, is this an ego need, or is it our mission?

Solar plexus is our personal power, and it's all organic. It holds most of our organs, the ones we use to assimilate our world. It's how you belong and commit to this world. It all starts with you. You are the pebble that creates a ripple effect in the water. Your ability to be yourself is what creates this effect. Great characters, such as the Dalai Lama, know themselves. They are free to be themselves no matter the environment and the circumstances. That is power, that is charisma, and attraction.

When these energy centers are balanced, you feel grounded, supported. We go to the ground floor. According to Caroline Myss, this is the first stage, where we work to be safe. Then we climb up to the second floor, where we start creating and start birthing ourselves. Then comes a stage where you feel confident, you know and trust your abilities. You have capacity, you have agency.

The zero point.

Your heart is the bridge between your base chakras and your upper chakras. We call it the Zero Point. It's where everything stabilises and you get back to homeostasis. It's where healing begins and ends. Your heart is where it all is. It's where you breathe (heart and lungs), it's where you grieve, it's where you clear the energies.

Your heart is a conduit for giving and receiving, income and outcome. The back part of your heart is about receiving, and the front part is about giving. Every chakra in your system has a front and back, but you must take a special look into your heart. It can build a wall over time or many lifetimes. Your karma is around your heart, as is your destiny. Love yourself, love others, and trust them. The heart works in conjunction with the solar plexus when you trust yourself and others. When you use judgment and compassion. It also works in conjunction with your throat chakra, when you speak your truth.

The upper chakras.

I believe our upper chakras are related to our conscious evolution.

Your throat chakra is related to your truth but also related to your devotion to self. Your thyroid is located in this energy center, and so is your thymus. Your high heart is right below your throat chakra, so they're connected. If, for example, in one past lifetime you neglected yourself, you put everyone else first, you become an over giver, and your heart is affected as well. All chakras are interrelated.

Your third eye is about trusting your psychic vision. So, when you close your eyes, what do you see? Now you're not using your eyes, but your inner eye. From there we move to the crown chakra, where your past lives converge. It's your connection to your DNA strand. Crown chakra is also your connection to your higher self.

Our base chakras are physical, emotional, mental, and spiritual too. Distortions can present in any chakra that is not balanced. That is why we talk about misalignments. We're connected from head to toe. Our chakras provide an energetic language to frame our energetic and spiritual work. Our body is the real gift.

So, all of your experiences ignite your mission and support your teachings. You can teach on many places and many levels, from your immediate family to your community. It doesn't have to be anything other than that. Then, you know you're on your mission. You stay in your heart and then connect to your intuition.

Part 2 - The Path of Change

Chapter 5 - Trusting Your Intuition

W e've spoken about the chakras and their respective energy. The way your energy body communicates with you in a unique way. But, what good does it make to have all this information if we don't actually listen to this inner guidance? Learning to trust our intuition is probably one of the most important tools of the Warrior, and one of the first steps towards change.

We live disconnected. From ourselves, for our energy, form our body, and from each other. We live too much in our heads. Overthinking, analysing, and then judging the results we achieve.

Our masculine and feminine energies are out of balance, and then we focus too much on what we do instead of focusing on what and who we are. We live constantly responding to what happens outside ourselves, completely disregarding what's going on inside.

Trusting our intuition means learning to be quiet and listen. Listen to our body, our energy, our feelings. Listening to our inner guidance and wisdom. Believing in our power, in our connection to the Divine. It's a practice, and it takes consistency. It's simple, but complex at the same time. It's simple because the practices are easy to do, but complex because as we do them, we uncover the layers that our soul wants to bring into awareness, so they can heal.

Let's discuss what intuition is, how to listen to it, and how to use it to connect to our mission and our service to others.

Your intuitive gifts.

If you're not new to spirituality, you have probably heard about psychic abilities and how they manifest differently in everyone. These gifts allow for those who have them (and we all have at least one) to perceive reality beyond their physical senses, with their third eye, their intuition. These may manifest as expanded versions of your five senses, so you can perceive visions, sounds, smells, or thoughts that give you information beyond the physical realm.

For example, when you go in meditation, or when you are in a relaxed state, you may get visions for your intentions, answers to the questions you're asking yourself, or powerful insights. This is clairvoyance. Sometimes you hear guidance loud and clear. A word, a direction, coming from your guides or your soul. It tells you to do something, call someone, go somewhere, very clear and specific guidance. This phenomenon is known as clairaudience. Other times, you are able to feel something, experience a strong emotion out of the blue, that is heading you in the right direction. That is clairsentience. When you know something in your heart, without analysing, when you "just know", you're experiencing claircognizance. For each sense and psychic ability, there's a "clair".

My main psychic intuitive abilities are clairaudience and clairsentience, but I've experienced all "clairs" and maybe so have you. One of the most interesting experiences was when I felt a clear taste in my mouth, something metallic, definitely not usual. Another time I experienced the smell of cigars and smoke coming out of nowhere. When this happens to me, especially when I'm with a client, it's hard to understand its meaning at the moment. So I ask my clients if my perception has some meaning to them. I've also experienced smells that remind me of a past event or a deceased one.

My clients also experience this. They smell flowers, like roses or lavender, when we call in their grandmothers. They can also sense familiar food smells that remind them of a place and time. They bring about memories. What's important with these experiences, is that you recognise them for what they are. Your spirit guides and your soul are bringing something to your awareness. Smell is the first sense that gets activated, so they use it often to bring messages. That is why aromatherapy is so powerful.

Your intuitive gifts and your psychic perceptions are subjective. Sometimes you'll have no words to describe their meaning because they speak to your subconscious. They bring about emotions, and our Western thinking model has taught us to disregard emotions, to ignore them. Emotions are very layered, entangled even, and have a language of their own. Not a language we learn easily. If we feel tired, or out of balance, we just ignore it. Until we can't ignore anymore, there's a deep soul urge to address. Then, the real intimate learning and connection to soul is developed. The soul connects through feelings.

That is why I love working with mothers. Imagine if they had the tools to support their children exactly the way they needed. Imagine if mothers treated themselves the way they deserved. That would help them be more grounded around their children, reflecting on them empowering emotions, sharing with them uplifting energy. Imagine them understanding that children have their own layers that need attention, and how their conscious understanding would help them evolve.

Distorted masculine and feminine energies.

It's difficult to listen to your intuition when you are out of alignment. We all hold the masculine and the feminine energy in us. When we overthink, over-analyse, we stay in our brains and block the connection to our bodies and our energy system. Most of us are familiar with the fact that modern society has a strong distorted masculine energy, but did you know that a distorted feminine may be getting in the way of listening to your intuition too?

When we have excessive masculine energy, we push, push, and push. We keep doing more and more, instead of allowing for flow and letting ourselves be pulled. You feel like there is not enough time, and you keep moving on to the next thing, and the next one, non-stop. When the feminine energy is excessive, you judge yourself. You do the opposite of being compassionate to yourself.

So, your distorted masculine keeps you working non-stop, and your distorted feminine judges the results you're getting after all the doing. And then it seems like it's never enough. Sounds familiar? You'll get angry. Not from a healthy perspective, but from suppressing guilt, shame, as you feel that you're never enough. It's ok to feel anger, but it's not supportive when it comes from judgment of who you are and what you do.

Balanced masculine and feminine energies will lead you to be present and trust the journey without judgment.

You need to slow down to speed up.

Using your intuition for healing - a simple practice.

Awareness is key. It is the starting point towards intuitive healing. First, Locate pain or discomfort in your body, as we've discussed before. Even if you're tired, or low in energy, which are sensations you feel all over the body, recognise them. Then, acknowledge these sensations, open the space for what they need to say, for what needs to come up to awareness.

The pain is signalling an underlying issue. That is what needs attention. That is what your body and emotions are bringing to awareness. It's all about acknowledging where you are, so you can then break the patterns and begin the path to change. That is where the process can get complex, because there are many underlying issues, one on top of the other.

I see this energy as a thick rope entangled and takes time, energy and focus to untangle the emotions attached, causing the discomfort. Disrupting the soul's path of alignment, balance, and peace.

You can access underlying core issues through an intuitive, sensational process. Yes, use your senses. Filter and engage each sense. What do you see? Eyes open and eyes closed?

What do you hear? What do you taste? What do you smell? What and where do you feel? This process is usually facilitated in a trance state going beyond conscious mind to access subconscious and unconscious bias. Where traumas from this lifetime and past lifetimes are held.

Conscious awareness is the key to healing.

Once you have sought awareness of the underlying issue, all you need to do is breathe into it. Give it some space. Breathe into the part of your body that is speaking to you. Your eyes, your feet, your back, your neck, wherever you feel the discomfort, visualise you sending your breath into that specific spot. Softly, consistently, in and out. Now, as you breathe, ask your body questions. How can I name this feeling? Is it pain, is it irritation? Let's say it's irritation, as an example. Now close your eyes and ask what's irritating? Is it management? Is it productivity? Is it a relationship? Is there too much noise in your head? Too much to do?

Once you have an answer, ask again. Go deeper. Trust the first answer that comes forward. For example, you discovered your headaches because there are too many thoughts in there. What's one of those thoughts? The first that comes forward it's bypassing your conscious mind, so that is the one. Trust the process. Then ask, what's the underlying emotion behind the thought? And then, underneath that emotion, are there any more thoughts? Keep asking questions until you feel everything you need to know has come to the surface. Until you've peeled as many layers as you can and uncovered the core wound. Breathe into the emotion. Relax the area where it's located. Put your hands on it and take deep breaths.

The work of uncovering the layers can be complex, but it helps us bring clarity and awareness. Discomfort may come back, but now you've removed all the thoughts that cover the underlying issue. Overthinking usually stops us from seeing what we need to heal and won't let us open space for it.

Another process I use to let go of the layers is I ask my intuition for colors. When you experience pain or discomfort, close your eyes. What color do you see? Each color relates to a different chakra, and that gives us a clue on where to start uncovering the layers.

Then give your body time to settle. Relax, let it come back to homeostasis. The body is very intuitive and knows the way. So just settle, settle, settle. Avoid putting pressure on yourself, and give yourself space instead. Let go of the stories you have created around your wound. Let go of your patterns, that's where the miracle lies.

Let go of the thought of what you need to do next, or what you need to accomplish next. Appreciate what you've achieved today instead. Stay in the present moment.

The power of supporting each other.

In my Circle, we use the phrase *hand to hand, heart to heart.* I want everybody to hold hands, and I want everybody to understand what it means energetically.

Relationships have healed by this simple yet potent gesture of soul, spirit connection of holding hands. We see hands being held in celebration, ceremony, life and death, deathbeds, but what if we held hands more while we can? What if we looked to share and connect with each other on a deeper level?

> ### *The most intimate thing you can do with another human is to hold their hand and show caring.*

Hands hold the energy of healing. They are a connection direct to the heart. It's the energy point for giving and receiving. We give with the right hand and receive with the left. When we have a deep connection with someone, we'll hold hands.

Holding hands is a symbol of belonging and commitment. Holding hands is just really beautiful, and we don't do it enough as adults, because it is intimate, and we are scared to be vulnerable. When I open my Circle there's a new level of appreciation for this close connection of hands and hearts. We feel safe, held, supported. We help each other heal. We release karma. Holding hands help you strengthen relationships, and reassure your sense of belonging. It takes courage to hold someone's hand.

When I hold your hand, I see you, and that may scare you. Most of us don't want to be seen, because we feel we are not perfect. But what if all that matters is that I see you just the way you are?

There's too much energy out there, too much information. We need support. We need that connection to help us feel anchored. When we come together, our nervous systems regulate each other. A group of people coming together in the same room, focusing on the same intention, will ignite powerful energies, healing energies.

This is what I call the cauldron. We all come into the cauldron in the center of the Circle, and then all the energies are distributed evenly so that there's calm. The energies recalibrate and they become a healing force.

Chapter 6 - Quantum Change

*T*here are many ways in which we can bring about change in our lives. Some people avoid change at all costs. Others take the long route by engaging themselves in doing things that they believe will bring change. They try to modify their environment through their doing. It's what we do best. We fill the space by adding more.

What if we didn't add, but released along the way? What could we release with ease? What needs some chipping away as without it, we feel lost, identity unknown? How do we change and have safety, security and confidence in this new space? Sometimes we have forced change too. Ideally we want incremental subtle shifts that become embodied and immersed on multiple levels e.g. mind, body, and spirit. We remember and reclaim all parts of us soul, spirit, and body. This is what I call quantum transformation. Slow and steady subtle shifts that all of a sudden become part of you.

What is quantum change?

Quantum change is a sudden, significant, and lasting transformation that would seem impossible from a limited mind's perspective. It requires little effort, but you need to do the inner work, which takes time. Quantum change happens instantly, as a sudden, seemingly mild shift inside of you, in micro-instances we don't often observe. Small, subtle changes start to accumulate into this significant shift. As you go inside, peeling the layers of your beliefs, you can have an unbelievable change as you uncover the narrative that limits you. Things can change really fast when you go through the quantum healing process if you take the time to do the inner work it requires.

A quantum shift will be a shift from your grounding where you are now, subtly shifting you. We start a quantum change when we set an inquiry. Your curiosity is the shift because if you can't be curious then your world of possibilities won't open. The quantum is big, expansive, and multi-dimensional. It's like space, like what you see when you look at the sky at night, full of stars, infinite. You can't make sense of it at first; you can't connect the dots as you look at the constellations. When you look behind, the dots are joined, just like what happens with the stars in one of those sky apps.

The same happens with quantum energy. You cannot see it with the naked eye, but you can feel it; you can sense it. There's an underlying vortex of creation that wants to come through. But we have to step into curiosity. We must ask ourselves constantly:

What's next?
What do I need to know today?

It's like having a mantra. Every day I ask myself, what do I need to know today? How can I be of service today? How can I show up? Please, guide me.

Quantum change also occurs when you make a conscious decision. In that moment something shifts. You will begin to see change.

Quantum shifts occur at the ego-mind level combined with soul- spirit level too. It's the combination of conscious decision making, trust and surrender that propels you toward your desired future self and all its potential.

What about illness? Will there be quantum leaps there too? Of course! You implode from the inside-out. Healing from illness has its own soul gifts. Something recalibrates from the inside-out. Providing courage and tenacity mixed with fortitude and humility. Surrender to the path ahead one step at a time. Illness (not that I would advocate this path) is a great awakener and has potential for the deepest and most expansive quantum shifts.

If illness presents in your life, you may ask for support, through conventional or non-conventional methods. One of them is that you seek out a healer. When you decide to go to a healer, that decision shifts something within you. That is the exciting bit. It's all about discovering what's new, what you can decide today. It makes you wonder. A quantum shift can be really subtle, and it can start with a decision; even if you think nothing is happening, it is. Do we have to wait for illness to create a quantum shift? No, we don't.

At this moment, we're undergoing a recalibration of frequency across the Earth. That means that lots of people are experiencing quantum shifts. It may happen to you if you get a headache out of the blue, your ears start ringing, or you get other physical signs. We live in a world where the code frequencies are changing. It's like an evolving currency. The way we react to things, the way we relate to others, it's all changing. But we won't see the changes come about until we feel safe and grounded. Releasing fear is a great part of the healing process and quantum change. The moment we let go of those fears and stories we keep telling ourselves, it's the moment we can get accelerated accomplishments.

We're used to living in fear and striving, not so used to thriving.

Feelings of safety vary from person to person. Each of us holds a different life experience, and that experience affects how we perceive reality. Unpacking that framework, that content of experience, allows a new level of understanding. It opens space for appreciation of everything that happens in our lives. Then you can feel safe, secure, and held.

The heart is the center where this expansion begins. If you go back to chapter 3, you'll see the image of the body quadrants, with the heart at the very center. The heart is where it all comes together. Faith, hope, love, and powerful healing emotions reside in the heart. The more you expand your heart, the more you can trust yourself and the world. The more you live from your heart, the safer you'll feel.

The transformation process.

Remember that transformation doesn't happen instantly, as if you were using a vacuum to get rid of all the thoughts, emotions, and stuck energy that doesn't serve you. Transformation is a process that you need to go through. Just as the tissues in your body have layers, so do your thoughts, emotions, and soul levels. Enlightenment is about peeling off those layers as they show up.

Be more instead of doing more.

Be more authentic, more present, more of who you are. Surrender to where you are and who you are right now. You can also plan for your future and see it clearly by being present. When you see it, you'll believe it, and it will come to pass. That is how surrender works. You don't need to know how this transformation will happen; all you need to do is pick up the breadcrumbs that come in your way and stay present.

If you take action in this state of surrender and presence, it will be inspired action. Even if it means just stepping outside to find a feather. You'll pick it up and say "thank you." This feather can be a message for you of gratitude, building your resilience, your foundation. Letting you know that you deserve to achieve what you put out in the world. You can now be open for guidance, not needing to understand how anything will come to pass; this is what surrendering is.

The awakening process.

The quantum shift happens with an awakening of some sort. That awakening can be an illness, it can be spontaneous, or even just a decision, as we've stated before. It changes our frequency. After this awakening, we go into a bliss state. You have made a decision, and it feels so good! You want to share what has happened to you; you want everyone to know. You get excited, and you begin to change. You start something new: a business, change of habits, whatever you feel called to do. And you just love it all.

Then comes the next stage, when you go into the Dark Night of the Soul. Your ego takes over. You start asking yourself questions like, *"Who do you think you are?"*. You start believing change is impossible or scary. And it *is*. Change can be scary. It makes us feel insecure. Some people will stop what they're doing. They will sabotage themselves. They buy into the stories that they can't be different. They can't be different from their families; they worry they won't belong anymore. They question if they commit; if this change is genuinely their soul's calling.

We have decided that we're going to change; we decided that we're going to create this business, create that mission, and take the following steps. The next step is we go into the void. We don't know how. We almost go into free-falling at this stage because the quantum is so big! We doubt ourselves and feel insecure about the steps we must take to move forward.

That is until you finally land and feel grounded. It's an inside job, and once you do it, you become grounded. You find your feet; you find your message, your clients. You practice being in this space. I used to practice being in business because practicing made me perfect, perfectly imperfect. I'm never going to be perfect, and neither will you. Because we're human, and humans are not perfect. That makes us unique because if we were perfect, we would be robots. Going to this last stage is mission and purpose. When we get there, no one can shake us. We've landed. It's our mission and our purpose.

Spirituality can really support us on this inspiring yet scary journey. It can dial down the chaos of the inside job we need to do. Once you do your work and evolve and take the steps, the quantum becomes like a circle around you, like a spider's web taking you over—a *web of wisdom.*

Intention in the process of quantum change.

An intention is focused energy. It's a strong pull towards what you want—the sensation in your energetic field of what you truly desire. Without intention, you won't change. And if you don't hold that intention into your sphere of reality, it won't manifest. Your sphere of reality is what you believe is possible, what you believe reality holds for you.

Yes, there are practical ways to get what you want, to heal, and bring change, like the **SMART** goals system (Specific, Measurable, Accountable, Realistic, Time-bound). But if you can't feel it in your heart, if you can't sensationalise those goals, they will never happen. Because it all begins with energy, embodiment, and sensation. Think of what you want. How does it feel? Get all your senses involved. How does it taste, sound, smell? How does it feel when you touch it? What do you see as you get what you want? This is the process of embodiment that gets that goal into your sphere of reality.

The process is simple: *dreaming it, believing it, achieving it.* You don't need to believe me; go gather your own evidence!

I teach my clients to set an intention and then forget about it. They all marvel as their intentions come true! I've seen it happen over and over again. We do intention-setting every month, and every month they materialise! Then we do a ritual around that materialisation. The whole process basis on the belief that you can do it, a belief that is almost a compulsion, a strong pull towards your intention.

Since we work with the natural laws, start by asking the question: *what's coming into my sphere?* You can set whatever intention you want. For example, I want to work with ten more clients. Then you sensationalise it. You embody it. How would it feel to work with these new clients? What do they look like? How do they speak? What is their energy like? Then, gather evidence.

Every time an intention comes to manifest, you are getting proof that the process works, which helps you grow your belief, allowing you to manifest even more intentions. It's an upward spiral.

We tend to cap our intentions based on our experience. We all work around a framework we know and feel comfortable with. But we won't manifest an intention unless we formulate thoughts around it. Those thoughts need to move outside that framework, outside our known reality, and into a new one. So, calling something into your sphere of reality means creating a new experience. It's fully embodying what you want so that it becomes part of your new reality.

Old thoughts may arise. Then you can say, *"Ok, thank you, brain. I know I'm doing something new, but let's put fear aside."* Then you do the rational part and take action. You dissect your dream into actionable steps and follow the process. That is how dreams come true!

When I decided I wanted to run New York Marathon, people used to ask me: *"Maria, how are you going to do that?"* and I used to answer: *"I don't know, I haven't done it yet. Let's find out."* But there was a firm intention—a soul calling to do it. I announced my intention and committed to it. I asked my coach to train me. We had a training program that I followed religiously. I got to the start line and then to the finish line. These are the processes that compose the dream.

Make a wish!

I often use the word wish instead of intention. There's no difference to me, but to people making a wish relates to magic. Magic is alchemy, the process of true, lasting change —achieving what seems impossible. Magic starts with a wish, with the art of asking.

A lot of people I work with don't know how to ask. How would you ask the Universe for something you want if there were no filters, no reframes? If you had no limitations at all? But what often happens is we ask ourselves: *Who do you think you are to ask for that?* There is an underlying element of not deserving what we wish for. That is when you tap into the power of community. As we support each other and see other members get what they want, we pay attention. *What did that person do? Can I do the same?* You follow the bread crumbs until you find your own way and flavour to ask and receive.

At the end of the day, it may be you sabotaging your ability to get what you want – the unconscious bias can be buried deep. So, first, you need to discover if underlying thoughts and fears are blocking your belief. The best way to find out is to ask your body. It never lies. You can use the pendulum, muscle testing, balancing, or any self-enquiry technique. The question here is to get a sense of the answer. Don't analyse it; feel it. After you decide what you want, ask yourself if you believe you have the capacity and the agency needed to bring that into your sphere of reality.

Let's use the example of you wanting to increase the number of clients you serve with your business. Do you have the time to tend to them appropriately? The capacity and agency needed to hold space for them? How do you want to work with them? What do you want to charge for them? Then, feel your energy. Feel the energy you need for that specific number to come into your sphere. If you feel you are not ready, you can either decide to adjust the goal or work around your beliefs to make that happen. This is the process of deconstructing a wish, which will keep you motivated. You can feel the energy of what you want moving; you are now seeing possibilities clearly.

Chapter 7 - Embodying and Grounding Change

*E*mbodiment happens when you let energies settle in your system when you absorb new frequencies and vibrations. Embodiment happens at multiple levels: physical, emotional, mental, and spiritual.

The first point of call you experience is visceral. Where do you feel the energy in your body? We've discussed this in earlier chapters. Then comes the mental level. The mind is attached to emotions, so they become the bridge between the physical and spiritual bodies. There are four layers in between. You may include the psychic level there too, but we'll leave it out for this book. At least for levels, I want you to understand that the embodiment process goes through.

That is why change is so difficult for some people or why it takes so much time for them. We all say that we don't have the time to feel, connect, and allow those energies to go through these layers consciously. There's too much noise out there, too much to do. But what if you did have time? What if you set your intentions and focus? How would your life change? No filter? No old paradigm filter?

This concept of pulling the energy is what we're working on. We're not pushing and pushing, your pulling things towards yourself. There's minimal effort involved. We're working on each energetic bridge between levels through embodiment.

First, you set an intention. Then, you ask, "where do I feel it in my body?". If you don't feel anything, you become aware of a disconnection. Come back to your body, listen, and observe. Is this intention true for you? It's a yes; come back to your body. Wake up that part of your body that is giving you that yes. It may take time to reconnect these intuitive sensations, but your pattern is there. There are cosmic responses, past life issues, or other energies that may need clearing. Are you willing to do that work?

Working to connect to your body is dance. Once you achieve it, you'll begin having amazing experiences once you get to that core. Maybe you will feel your heart space first, then your throat. Then you'll identify the emotion you're feeling in your throat; you'll be able to name it. Is that emotion attached? Is it linked to a thought? Now you're moving one more level into your mental body. And then you finally move to the spiritual. You understand and see the root causes of these sensations without judgment. You may feel they make no sense in the beginning. Still, eventually, as you continue with the work, you begin to ground and set a foundation, starting with your body, emotions, and thoughts.

Grounding change.

The process of grounding anchors you to Earth, a powerful magnifier and supporter for your wish or intention. It's a powerful process because Earth is matter, and that is how you materialise your dreams and bring them into this plane of existence, corresponding to the physical body which also matter. Grounding is another type of embodiment process. Change means getting out of your comfort zone, so it is, by definition, an uncomfortable process. Many people resist change. But if you embody the process, it'll catapult you into a new reality, it's a whole different experience.

Superficial spiritual teachings will ask you to think about a goal. They'll instruct you to repeat your wish x number of times. That is a starting point, for sure, but it will take you nowhere without embodiment. If you stay at the level of thought, other thoughts will come, and you'll place them on top of the intention. If a thought doesn't make sense to you, you won't bring it into your sphere of reality.

Embodiment is a cellular process. I'm no physicist, but I'm a psychic. I can see energy. Words have energy. If you look at the energy attached to any word you're using, you will know when it will come to fruition. It will give you goosebumps. You *just know* it's going to happen. And then, if you take action, there's truth to it. Divine truth will surround it. But keep in mind that, as humans, we need to take action as well.

We have spoken before about my client, who had been diagnosed with trigeminal neuralgia, causing her extreme and constant pain. When she came to me, she asked a simple yet powerful question: *How do I heal from this?* Hers was a long-term chronic illness. While working together, we found the core element she needed to address. At that time, she was also writing a book as her legacy. Part of her legacy to her family was her healing process. Without consciously knowing, she was building a body of evidence. The book became the registry for her healing path. She could then see that her body was responding to the healing process. The evidence was there. In the same way, she came up with a book out of nowhere; through a creative process, she was also healing.

Throughout the process, she experienced setbacks; there were days when she felt discomfort and pain. Still, as she kept writing, she saw the overall progress. Her condition had been there for years. Her intention, desire to be curious and try different things, and her will to gather evidence of her progress, allowed her to heal.

Change your experience.

*You know what you know until you know
something different.*

Once go through something new, it becomes part of your experience. If you tried something that didn't work, that gets stuck in your subconscious, sometimes as a block. But you must keep trying. Practice something different; see what happens this time. Find the healing modality that works for you and stick to it. Be curious, your body and mind will adapt, and your soul will guide you. No one solution will work for everyone, so you must find your own.

A good spiritual teacher will set a line of inquiry that is new to you. One that resonates on some level, but cognitively, it doesn't land. That is the work that is changing the world from the inside out. I firmly believe that when the student is ready, the teacher will appear.

Gathering evidence is a way to build belief but also a way to practice. *I tried that. How did that feel? I felt lighter!* And then your body will recognise what works and what doesn't. Eventually, over time, the process of change becomes spontaneous. Most likely, you'll have to keep doing some work around it as you peel more and more layers that need healing. But you will build on it. You will develop an "energetic muscle." When you discover what works for you, you're building a body of knowledge. This is what I like to call "your toolbox." I always encourage my clients to explore and discover what works for them instantly and add it to their toolbox.

One of the easiest tools I recommend for embodiment is using breathwork. It will work instantly for most people. Any type of breath will help. You can use yogic techniques, shamanic breath, or even just inhaling, holding your breath, and slowly exhaling. Breath is your life force; if you can expand that life force, that is your magnitude in the world.

Spiritual laws of nature.

I use the Spiritual Laws of Nature in my work. They are also known as Hermetic principles. They are ancient, millenary wisdom used by many ancient civilizations before us, such as the Egyptians and the Greeks. These principles are not related to religious beliefs but are more like metaphysical principles by which the universe operates. There are lots of resources about these laws. For this book, I'll briefly describe them and then explain how I apply them to my work and how they help you manifest and ground lasting change.

1. *The Law of Mentalism.* All is mind; the universe is mental. Everything we experience, including emotions, thoughts, energy, and the physical experience, are thoughts of a living Mind.

2. *The Law of Correspondence.* As above, so below; as below so above. As within, so without; as without, so within. This principle embodies the notion that micro and macro are the same, that there are patterns that repeat themselves endlessly, and so what happens on what level impacts the other.

3. *The Law of Vibration.* Nothing rests. Everything moves. Everything vibrates. The universe is always in motion. Everything that exists is nothing but different frequencies of vibration. Thoughts also have different levels of vibration.

4. *The Law of Polarity.* Everything is dual and has poles. These opposites are identical in nature but different in degree. Extremes meet in a reconciled paradox. Opposites are nothing but sides of the same coin, perceptions of degree. For example, prosperity and scarcity are degrees of abundance. At exactly which degree of abundance do you stop perceiving scarcity and move into prosperity? The Law of Polarity explains this paradox.

5. *The Law of Rhythm.* Everything flows in perfect cycles. Life has its ups and downs, highs and lows. The universe is in constant motion, moving from one polarity to another,

constantly changing. Understanding this principle helps us embrace the transitory nature of all things and experiences. No matter how good or how bad your situation, it will pass. You will then enter another cycle.

6. *The Law of Cause and Effect.* Also known as the Law of Karma. There is a consequence for every action and every thought. Life events are not the product of chance; everything happens for a reason. This principle is closely related to the power of setting intentions and conscious action.

7. *The Law of Gender.* The masculine and feminine energies are inside everything and everyone. Feminine and masculine principles are manifest on all planes of existence. Our creative power is based on this Law. The masculine is assertive, competitive, and achieving. At the same time, the feminine is receptive, nourishing, and allowing, and both of them are necessary. Both of them must exist in perfect balance.

Understanding how the universe works help us get more grounded in our journey. They can give us more clarity in our path to healing. I work with my clients to understand and apply all these principles. Of course, each individual case will require the entrainment of one or another, but there are some of them that I use at the core of my practice.

Applying the Law of Correspondence.

I work a lot with the Law of Correspondence. *As within, so without*, states this Law. The inner work you do will affect your outer experience. It also equates to the reticular activating system for our consciousness. What you intend, you see. As you become conscious of your intentions and you begin to embody them, manifestations of these will show up in your life.

Understanding this principle is about activating the inner wisdom that anything is possible, so long as we believe in it. It's precisely that belief (or the lack of it) that trips us up. We fall again into the trap of the inner dialogue and the societal narratives. *"Who do you think you are?"* This is what you may ask yourself when you first set your intention. You have set a ceiling on your dreams only because of your unconscious bias. By removing those inner dialogues and beliefs, you're changing from the inside out. Your external reality will reflect your internal state.

"As above, so below. As within, so without."

You can't achieve what's not in your scope of reality. To achieve something, you must believe it is possible. You likely know what you don't want; but, are you clear about what you want? Because if you are not, you won't allow yourself to experience it. Your reality within must match your intentions, and then they will manifest in your outer reality. You have been struggling. You are tired of feeling sad, anxious, worried, and stressed. You want to feel better on the inside, but you are scared that if you open up Pandora's box, it will only make things worse. But the truth is, there is nothing you can't overcome. You won't get to the light unless you go through your darkness.

Chapter 8 - Stepping Into Darkness

When we desire something, we set an intention. The Law of Mentalism says the Universe is mental. So, all we manifest begins with a thought. As you place your attention and energy on that thought, it becomes an intention. You start to call it in.

Every time we call something into our reality, we call it fully, including its light and shadow. Everything has a duality. As we studied in the previous chapter, according to the Law of Polarity, opposites are manifestations of one thing, but to different degrees. They are sides of the same coin. For example, as I teach freedom to my clients, they connect to their desire for freedom and liberation. With that intention comes the realisation of all the things that keep them from experiencing freedom. We all need to see the darkness so the light can shine.

The seed needs to go into darkness, deep down into a connection with the Earth. It's in that shadow that it grows. If you plant a seed, you will allow it to have a space in the darkness. You know and trust there is growth. You understand that it may need care, nurturing, and attention. Your intentions are seeds, and you plant, nurture, and watch them grow.

We may be in the light now, but we will need to face the darkness if we want to keep growing. This cycle will repeat itself as long as we commit to peeling all the layers of our subconscious.

Learning to embrace your darkest moments.

Most spiritual teachings out there say that embracing the darkness means lowering your vibration and that you shouldn't pursue that. Others, bypassing spiritual teaching, will deny darkness completely by saying that it is an illusion. They teach you that you won't have to face darkness if you vibrate at the right frequency. I believe those ideas are dangerous. If you are experiencing a period of darkness, or if that is all you know, you'll start believing there is something wrong with you, that you're not good enough. If you live under that self-judgment narrative, there's no energy to explore new options, to discover what else is out there.

But if you know there is a Law of Polarity, that everything holds both the light and the dark, even on the deathbed, towards the end of your life, you'll see the calm before the storm. There is a surge of energy before someone dies, then a release, followed by the renewal that death is. We can see this process as a human quality: first, a big surge of energy, then allowing, and finally, entering a void. That void is what we call darkness. We are programmed to avoid the darkness, but when you recognise it, when you accept it, you develop the tools to cope with it, to face whatever this emptiness brings to you. It then feels spacious.

Once we recognise and open that space, we need to nourish our bodies. It needs time to adjust. It needs nurturing. That is the rhetoric of self-love and self-care. Once we know our unique needs, we can recognise that duality, that polarity that comes along. Whatever comes, and however it shows up, we can now see it as a challenge, as an opportunity to pause, learn, and carry on.

Most of us do not know what we want. No one taught us to ask for what we want. We are trained extensively to repel what we don't want. For example, if I wanted to call in, say, $50,000; what would come up? I don't have $50,000. What would I do with it? I then would begin to experience the polarities that come from asking for that sum of money. For the money to materialise, I would need to see what's inside of myself and work on it. I'd act according to the Law of Correspondence: "as within, so without." I can now see both the darkness and the light and work on stories that won't allow me to receive the money. Am I worth it? What will I offer people to receive the money? Am I good enough? Most of us struggle with self-worth. "Who do you think you are?" is a recurrent question when we try to manifest something. However, you are expanding into your rightful position in life: the one you choose. There are no right, wrong or even levels. There is an inherent prosperous right to live a life in right livelihood. Free from impediments, open to curiosity, and wonder with ability to take inspired action as you navigate possibilities.

Growing is about learning to find that balance between your desires and the darkness they bring. Overcoming the objections that come from your body, mind, soul, and your spirit. You become aware of the stories you have been told for years, your programs, family history, and societal narratives. It is an internal mechanism, not external. When darkness shows up, it's a good thing. It means we can heal it. If stays buried in the dark, you will never see it, and it becomes a heavy unconscious bias to carry around with you.

Common narratives that show up in the darkness.

As you face the darkness, you will learn to identify the narratives that go in your head. They will depend on your circumstances, but they will help you identify and bust some myths. The strongest myth we face during our dark periods is the "I am not good enough" myth. Your inner dialogue will tell yourself: "Who do you think you are?" "That is not possible."

The Good Girl narrative is also prevalent. This one relates to our inability to say no. The Good Girl tries to get approval from others, so she'll say yes to everything that is asked of her; it's the inner child seeking validation. We hold this narrative also as a collective. That is why boundaries are essential.

The good girl narrative feels like emptiness. It's always giving us reasons why we can't do as we please or get what we want. I've seen it with my clients. I've experienced it myself, and I've fallen for it. It implies giving away all of yourself to others.

The opposite of this narrative is to love yourself enough to put yourself first. That is why I work with concentric circles. When you do the work of loving yourself enough, you come back to yourself, bring all of your parts together, let go of the Good Girl narrative and understand that you are good. Everyone is good. We don't need to prove anything nor seek approval.

You don't need to be happy all the time.

I want to debunk the myth that the way we feel depends on our connection or disconnection from Source. Once I met another healer who told me all she did was connect to Source, and then she'd feel good. I used to think there was something wrong with me because I could not experience the same thing. The truth is, no matter how we feel, Source is always supporting us. No recalibration is required. The experience of connecting to Source means different things for different people.

I teach and work with large groups of people. I hold space for all of them. After performing a ceremony, I raise so much energy that my body needs some adjustment. I sometimes wake up the next day with a hangover. That used to fill me with dread and anxiety because I thought I was doing something wrong. But I've learned, over the years and with cumulative experience, that this is just the way I process energy.

I want you to discover and respect your own process. Do a little research, and find out what others do. You will see it's different for everyone. Don't judge your process. I also want to debunk the myth that healing is just plugging into Source, without the awareness of the emotions that need to be processed. I don't want you to deny what you feel. It's important to follow the process of tuning into your body and exploring what your emotions tell you instead of just ignoring them and covering them under an artificial idea of happiness.

As you grow, you are traveling inter-dimensionally; you are crossing energetic borders, which requires some time and energy to adjust and recalibrate. Because, as you experience quantum change, you are going beyond the realm of your current reality, which requires some adjustment.

Experiencing other realms and astral traveling.

Part of the process of spiritual growth is allowing your soul to have the experiences it needs. Sometimes we get scared because these experiences seem out of the "normal," and we want to feel safe. Many people have out-of-body experiences or astral travel as they grow. They move to other dimensions through their dreams as well. I wish to acknowledge this process as part of the growth we do unconsciously. When we validate these experiences, they can open our vision and help us become a better version of ourselves here on Earth.

Astral travel can be prevalent for adults as well. Maybe you can't sleep, and you're woken a lot; this may be caused by astral traveling. Many women in the pre-menopausal state may experience this more frequently. Much of our spiritual journey is experienced unconsciously; meaning, outside of our conscious awareness. These experiences are unseen, yet you can sense them on many levels, including your mental and physical bodies.

When we do ancestral work to connect to our elders or our legacy, we start with the people we remember. Still, you can move five hundred to a thousand years back in time, or even more. As you do this, you are traversing energy, moving through the quantum field. It's the same with the ascension process. It takes time and work, but it can be done.

I hold circles because that connects us to the sphere, a field that can contract and expand, allowing us to have the experience we need or that we are looking for to heal and grow.

Healing the Mother Wound.

The Mother Wound can be a body of work on itself. Working on the Mother Wound is essentially healing your matriarchal lineage and what they taught you and your mother. Your mother will teach you the "yeses" and the "nos" in the world, and sometimes the powerful "nos" are your biggest teachers. They're the ones that interrupt your passion, your energy flow.

Healing the Mother Wound is work we all need to do since we all have a mother. If you try to recall your memories, you'll remember there were times when your mother ignored you or when she wasn't there for you in the way you needed or expected. We all experienced that at one point or another in our lives. We are all human, and we experience our own worries and struggles. Your mom was no exception. The crisis, the fears, and the struggles, she passed them all to you.

Many emotions may be attached to the Mother Wound. There can be shame, fear, or guilt. The way to heal it is through compassion. When you realise you did your best with the knowledge you had at the time, and so did your mother, you begin to heal. As you do this work, you are healing yourself and encouraging others to do the same. When we do this work together, we can go up to seven generations before us and heal from their past experiences. And you will also free seven generations to come. It works like a chain.

I love working with mothers because as soon as they build a foundation of compassion, kindness, love, and nurturing towards themselves, they are healing many generations. I work on concentric circles with the symbol of the sacred cells. Their work impacts their immediate circle and then the collective. It's the Law of Correspondence in action. It all starts when they feel supported, and they can move to compassion. That is how we heal the Mother Wound.

Part 3 - The Warrior

Chapter 9 - Working on Abundance and Money Narratives

*T*here are whole different narratives about money. They've been turned into books, courses, and coaching programs. We seem to be obsessed with this topic. It seems that is all we hear everywhere: "money, money, money…" But I want to distill it to its simplest form: if we're going to function at the level we want, and if we want a certain quality of life, we need currency. That is the way our society is built; we use money as a tool to acquire a certain lifestyle.

You can have all the money you want and need without judgment. All the mental blocks we experience around manifesting it or receiving it come from our narratives. Once you know that you are universally supported to thrive and look for tangible evidence of that support, your life changes. That is why you do a gratitude journal. So you start gathering evidence of the support you receive, and you become aware of it. It has always been there.

Your life can change with every small action you take to build that connection of universal support. When you light a candle for your intentions, knowing it symbolises an opportunity to see and reflect your light, your life changes.

When you embrace your children with deep love, even when you have a million things to do, your life changes. It changes with that commitment to contribution, and your capacity and agency expand to make a better world.

Now that you are clear and confident of that support, you can start working on healing your money narratives. Decide which one will you work on first. You can't work on them all at once; you need to choose. Most of them will fit in one of the three pyramid vertexes: time, energy, and money.

These are the three elements of our currency. If you don't have enough time to do what you need, you might become overstressed, overwhelmed, and it's hard to move forward, causing stress on your body. You won't enjoy life fully, including your money and the experiences you can create with it. If you don't have enough energy for what you want or need to do, this can be the beginning of energy dysfunction or even autoimmune disease. In my work I have seen this often. If you don't have enough money to have a quality life that you strive and thrive for, you might have heartbreak, heart disease, or even cancer. Those illnesses can come from living in scarcity. This, of course, is relative to each person but is what I've seen as a medical intuitive.

Become conscious of what you're working on. Set a clear intention. What is it that I want? Do I want to work on bringing more money? Or do I believe I need to work on my boundaries for time and energy? Do I need to rest and recharge? Do I have difficulty doing that? You can also set an intention to have more energy. Do I need to move my body more or take better care of myself? What is it that I need or want? Listen to your intuition, but distill it down to time, energy, or money and work on one.

I suggest you do this work with the help of a mentor or a coach. The process can be both fun and eye-opening. As you begin to distill what you want, ask yourself:

What does energy mean to me?
What does time mean to me?
What does money mean to me?

You begin to move your wishes from the ethers into manifestation. But you need support to build the scaffolding. You cannot do it alone. In my experience, personal and with clients, it is extremely difficult to navigate the dark, blind spots on your own.

Self-worth, value offer, and pricing.

Many people often struggle to define their value and, therefore, their prices. As they try to sell their products and services, get promotions or negotiate contracts; they often come up with objections and subjective comments from the people around them. Such as: *"You should give that service for* free" or "I wish I could afford your prices," or "I can get what you offer somewhere else at a lower cost." It is easy to fall into fearful patterns, question their value, and believe no one will ever buy from them. In my experience, this is a narrative that comes up every time an entrepreneur increases their prices.

You can choose to respond to these people or go inside and do the work around your worth and the value of what you do. We live in an economy based on value, so it's important to begin exploring by asking yourself:

What do I value and why?
What about money and value has been tarnished?

Our society has made us believe that the potency of money is only for the few, but guess what? You can build the capacity and the agency to receive any money you want. So don't let others project their unmet wounds onto you. You are now working on shifting; you are now a different person, as long as you can understand your value and the value of what you do.

Decide what your currency is. Is it relational? Is it emotional? Respect your currency and the currency of others. Then you are ready to set your pricing. This process can be uncomfortable initially, especially if you've decided to raise your prices. Many of the people I coach say: "But if I raise my prices, I'll break my business!" Stand firm - when the first person buys from you at your new pricing you start gathering evidence because you know your value and have experienced a tangible exchange. Then you start building capacity.

The Warrior knows and deserves life quality.

As healers, we may carry many societal narratives regarding our right to have and create money. This comes from many lifetimes. The Worrier may get entangled with some ancient premise of what it takes to live in the world, the quality of life they deserve, or what they should desire. You decide what quality of life means to you. No one else can set up that measure. It's a personal and empowered decision. The Warrior understands this and sets clear intentions.

The moment you are born, the stars literally align and dictates how you will be in the world, not as a prediction, but as information that can be insightful. Your astrological chart is filled with useful information that can empower you. Self-knowledge helps you work on yourself, on your shadow elements. You can better work on the weaknesses you have and work on your strengths. When you recognise and know those strengths, you celebrate them. We're rarely taught to celebrate our strengths; we always focus on our weaknesses and work on or judge them. The western mindset is about staying anchored in our shortcomings, stuck in a loop. We're not taught to accept ourselves deeply.

That is why the personal development industry has grown exponentially in the West. People know they want more; they need to grow and become a better version of themselves. But they don't want to see the dirt they encounter as they go deep into their darkness. They need a hand; they just can't see.

Wisdom teachers will step up and tell their stories. A better world will come afterward, creating a better legacy for future generations.

We tend to bury our pain. There's so much entanglement in our wounds! But when we hear someone else share their story, we begin to unravel ours. We question what happened to our mom, our grandma, our ancestors, and how it's impacting us. Understanding and owning our story can set us free. We begin a healing process that affects generations past and to come.

My money story.

My money story begins with my parents. They came to Australia from a village in Italy, and they were immigrants. They owed the cost of their voyage when they got here, so they were in debt as soon as they landed in Australia, a new country. Mom and Dad didn't speak the language, so they had no voice here. They worked hard to clear their debt. As a result, I've worked hard to find my voice and recognise my place in the world, always asking if I belong. My parents' values are with family, so I believe family comes first.

When I had money, I used to overspend it, or give it away. That pattern came from my parents working hard, clearing debt and then looking for opportunities to grow and expand, bringing them back into debt – a cycle was born. So, another of my money narratives is *"If I don't work hard, I cannot make money."* And what does hard work mean? It means giving all of myself away. An interesting narrative: *"If I can't keep money and I need to give all of myself away, then I can't retain money."* I've had to shift the concept of money to value and work on my worth and self-esteem.

What must I do to heal those narratives? I needed to belong and have a voice in a crowded and noisy industry. I created a platform where I am a wisdom teacher, using my voice to share my knowledge. That heals a part of my family story too.

I have also worked on balancing the way I give and receive money. I forgave myself for my old patterns. I focused on gaining financial independence as a legacy skill for my children and a way to show leadership. Then I started to manage my money, which at the time was new to me. As a kid, I had all my basic needs covered, but I didn't have the social activities that my counterparts at school had. I couldn't aspire for opulence or anything I desired. Who was I to do so? I wasn't working hard, so I didn't deserve it. That was my narrative back then, a scarcity mindset.

I come from a family lineage that worked hard to earn a living. They performed physical tasks such as toiling the land, operating machinery, or doing similar jobs. My work isn't hard in that sense. It is educational, intellectual, and philosophical. That wasn't deemed as hard work in my family. I had to gather evidence of the value of my work, making it tangible and quantifiable. Worth and value balance each other. I had to ask myself, *"How much can I receive for what I do?"*

I did market research on similar solutions, then did an energetic audit on myself and set a price point for my work. To get to that number, I had to collect evidence of my value. I looked at what value my work had brought to the people who worked with me. I saw how they found love after failed relationships, healed from diseases, made money, and increased their energy so they could do more. I saw how I helped them through their darkest moments, not only to survive but to thrive. It all gave me lots of joy. What value can you put on transformation?

This is work that lasts a lifetime. I've been teaching for over a decade. I have witnessed many transformations, mine included, and know what it takes to walk the path of wholeness, integration, and freedom. I don't take this work lightly. It is deep and it is sacred. Being well prepared and supported is a winning formula.

Comparisonitis.

Comparisonitis is a term I use to describe our compulsive need to compare ourselves to others. This need may come from imposter syndrome, good girl narratives, abandonment, betrayal, shame, or the mother wound. There are many layers entangled in our need to compare ourselves to others. People will tell you not to do it, but how can we stop comparing? We don't know any different. Here's a funny story.

As you already know, I used to run when I was in my early forties. I would run with a sixty-plus-year-old, just doing social running. As we did so, I used to watch other runners and start comparing myself to them. How they looked, how fast they were. And then, I began judging myself for not being as good. I was comparing my insides with their outsides. But then, every time we ran past someone looking perfect, my running partner would come close to me and whisper *"dry vagina,"* and I'd start laughing. It was her way of telling me that, even if something looks perfect on the outside, you don't know what's going on on the inside.

That is why *comparisonitis* makes no sense. Every time you find yourself in this comparison habit, remember we can't see the whole picture. We don't know what's going on inside. Apply this to looks and money, business, success, relationships, anything. Never judge yourself or others.

You have the freedom of choice. Your journey is about becoming the best you can be by practicing and dedicating yourself to what you love. Good runners are committed to running. Good healers are dedicated to their craft, to healing. Good magicians practice. And good coaches are dedicated to self-development.

Chapter 10 - Capacity and Agency

When you experience the evidence of new a reality forming, you move beyond limitations. You identify your soul's calling.

When I decided to become a millionaire, I looked, and I said: *"Oh my goodness! I'm already a millionaire!"* I was blessed with abundance on many levels. And I can see that because it's tangible. But what if I go to the realm of an unknown reality? That is where you look for new experiences. I then move one step further and begin wondering once more. I wonder what it would be like to be a multimillionaire. I haven't had that experience yet.

I know no one in my immediate reality who is a multimillionaire. So I start looking for proof that it is possible, and I begin making that reality tangible to me. What did multimillionaires do to have that experience? Let's find out.

Who do I need to become to experience that?
What resources do I need to gather?

Then, I take the following steps. If this is something that I really want, I will challenge myself because some of the narratives that don't belong to me will come out. We get so many stories!

This process is what I call building your capacity and agency to be more, do more, give more, and receive more. It is an expansive process that comes with inner work. Because with every expansion, comes its polarity. You will doubt and ask yourself again, "who do you think you are?"

When we work as healers or coaches in the self-development and spirituality space, we work with leadership and soft skills. As a leader, you must know that your inner child will sometimes come out, make you doubt yourself, and trip. So, watch out. Notice the thoughts coming in. Because when you feel physically and emotionally tired, you'll need to look after yourself.

Getting support.

Everyone has the capacity to create their own magic. They just have to gather evidence and get support. We cannot do it on our own. It doesn't matter how influential you are; you need people around you to be both a witness and be witnessed to expand your sphere of reality. As others grow their capacity and agency, it feeds yours. As they support you, you gather evidence of your success, and that is a unique opportunity.

Exploring your capacity feels good. Knowing your agency makes you grow and builds trust in yourself and others. You don't need to compete with anyone, but you can compete with yourself if you feel fuelled by a bit of competition. How do you do that? As you overcome each challenge in your way. When you are challenged, you're competing to expand. Even if they're uncomfortable, your struggles can be good for you. They're all bricks on your new path as you pave your way. And this road is always easier if you don't walk alone. Getting the support of those trying to achieve what you want and expand the same way will make it easier and certainly more fun!

Building your capacity.

At this point in the book, you are well aware of the stories that drive our thoughts and decisions and why and how we must overcome them. Once we become aware of our stories, we want to move away from them, and this process is very similar to grief. There are five stages to grief, and the first thing we'll do is reject these stories and deny them. Then we get angry at our family, our lineage. We may even wish we weren't born to these patterns. We then bargain with ourselves to find a way out that doesn't require as much inner work. Sadness and depression come next. We believe we'll never be capable of overcoming such deeply seeded beliefs and behaviours. We sometimes struggle with change, taking two steps forward and one step back. In the final stage of the process, you learn to accept your stories, see them with compassion, and let them go. They no longer have any power over you, and now you have expanded. You have evolved.

Building your capacity is an evolutionary process. It's about letting go of those stories and stepping into the unknown. It is also about gathering the evidence as you move forward on your inner journey and consistent actions. But you can't go from zero to a hundred in just one step. You need to build it. It's like running a marathon.

If I wanted to run a marathon tomorrow, and that is 42.2 kilometres or 26.2 miles – it would be impossible. My body isn't trained for that. But if I decide I'll run it in a year, I know I can. I've done it before, and others have done it too. The body has a memory, so I'm certain I can do it. But I need to be disciplined and commit to doing the work to train my body again.

It's the same with money and building a business. If I say that I'm going to have ten clients in one day and I'm only serving one at the moment, I'm going to be exhausted. I don't have the capacity to be of service to that many people. But I could say that within three months, six months, or even twelve months, I would like to build the capacity to serve ten a day. Or I could decide that ten a day is really extraordinary, so I could settle for ten a week, which would be more tangible.

Now my intention will manifest because I'm building up the muscle, I'll grow from one to three to ten. It is building that muscle and capacity. Before I know it, I will get there. It may take time, or maybe it will happen really fast, but what matters is that I collect the evidence to support that I can do it and that I can keep going and keep growing. There will be moments when I might drop off, but I can build myself up again anytime because I've got proof that I can do it.

That is precisely the same process our bodies go through to get stronger. Muscle fibers need to break down to build up. It's the same in business. We set the intention, build up, break down, and then build up again. There is no such thing as success or failure, no right or wrong. You need not worry. Thinking in terms of success and failure is what keeps us stuck. I now know better to recognise that success or failure, this too shall pass. Emotions and feelings, they all pass, and all we need to do is breathe. Tomorrow will be a new day, and what we do is enough.

Always keep this in mind as you build and grow your business. Anytime we are building something new, a new offer for our clients, a new launch, or a course or product, we grow our capacity, which can be uncomfortable. We are tired at the early stages of our latest launch because we've invested time and money on something that isn't selling yet. Then we work on our offerings and promotion, and still no results. We start judging our behaviour and our client's behaviour, and we may feel like giving up. We are too exhausted, seeing no results, and it seems like it's not worth it. Giving up seems easier, comfortable. Those are the moments when we must stay committed to our mission.

Your purpose is bigger than you.

If you feel like you can't go, keep up, and get support!

Building up your agency.

Agency is power in your knowledge; it is how you step into your reality and overcome your challenges. What service are you providing to the world? Where do you see yourself within that particular service?

Knowing what you do and why you do it gives you power.

Agency is about power, wisdom, and connection. You won't become a leader unless you step into the extraordinary, and I mean exceptional for your standards, for your experience.

You must be an example for others to follow. I believe leaders are an inspiration, even if they look scared or a bit lost at times. They are opening a new path for others to follow, gathering evidence that something completely new is possible.

As I grow my agency, I become a model for my children. They have seen me struggle, but they have also seen me build a business from scratch and evolve. I've done it, so now they know they can do it too. They can make decisions easily and go after their dreams because that is what momma has done. Am I scared at times? Yes, I'd even say a lot of the time. There are days when I want the give up. But there are also days when I celebrate my wins as well.

Building your capacity and agency requires discipline and a commitment to your mission. But you also need to celebrate every single step you take forward.

Connect, commit, and contribute.

I often give talks on cultivating the three C's: connection, commitment, and contribution. Cultivating to me is about seeding, observing, and being curious. On each of the steps, always observe with an inquisitive mind. Connection has three levels: how do you connect with yourself? How do you connect to those you serve? And, how do you connect to the collective? The same three questions apply to commitment and contribution in the form of concentric circles.

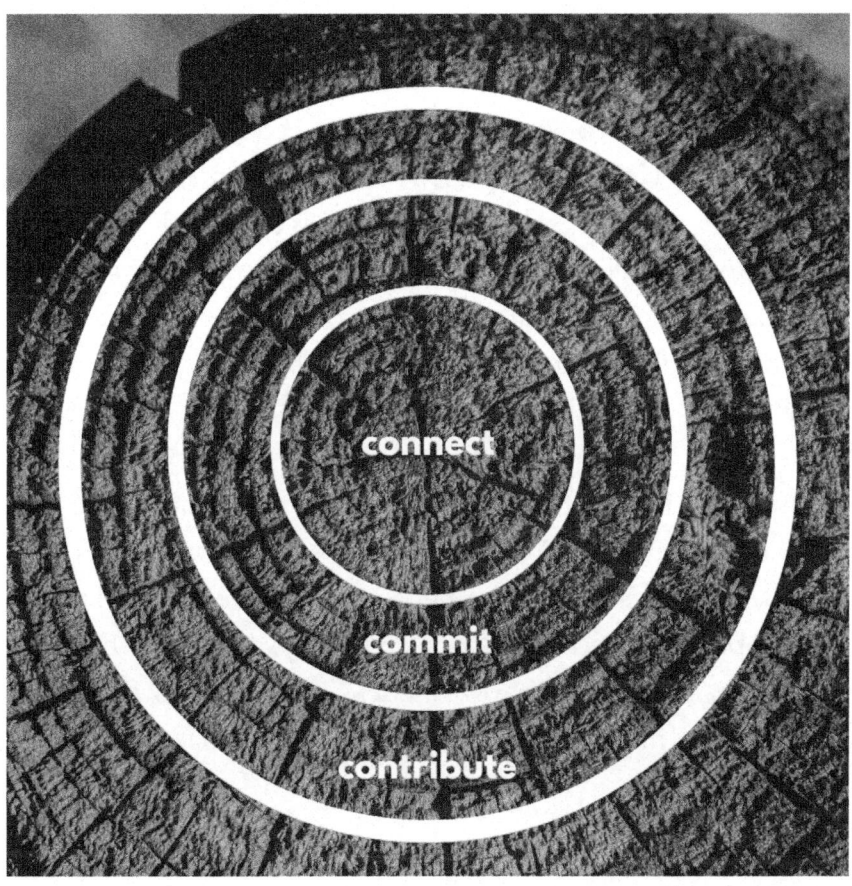

These layers compose a sphere operating in all time and space. Once you know how this concept unfolds inside of you, the external will follow. Your mission is bigger than you; just keep connected to it. Use it as motivation.

You can observe these spheres and move up and down the scale by the law of polarity. So, the opposite of connecting is disconnection. Feeling disconnected from yourself or the world around you, disconnected from your purpose. The opposite of commitment would manifest as a lack of discipline or inconsistency. To me, contribution means completion. Unless you use your gifts and business to contribute to the collective, your work will never be complete. You will never fulfil your mission. The opposite of contribution is believing you have nothing to give and aren't worthy of completion. But we are all here to contribute on some level.

Completion is perfectly symbolised in the shamanic work of soul fragmentation. You bring back those fragments that your soul has lost until you become complete. Completion is death, but it's also birth. It's creativity; it's bringing back your soul to wholeness, to oneness. And that is also what contribution means.

Your soul's true mission.

Your soul's first and most important mission is to look after yourself. We are not taught to do that. We're doing the exact opposite most of the time: we look after everybody before ourselves. That was me for a long time. I was brought up the way my mom was, her mom, and all the women from generations before us. I had to do my work to deconstruct this and many other stories that would allow me to grow my capacity and agency and connect, commit and contribute. Everyone is inherently good, but their stories take over, impeding them from connecting and moving outside the concentric circles.

Chapter 11 - Warrior Practices

You've come a long way through.

You've learned what healing means, how your energetic system works, and how to listen to your body and intuition. You now understand familial and societal narratives and how they impact your thoughts, beliefs, and actions.

You've moved from the "fix-me" mentality, stepped into your darkness, and committed to evolving. You've faced your stories and stepped into quantum change. You are now connected to others, your mission, and your soul's calling.

You are now beginning to live as a Warrior.

But it doesn't end here. The Warrior understands that evolution is an ongoing process. She is not afraid of it; she is willing to step into her power and do the work. And so are you. So in this chapter, I want to share with you some of the day-to-day practices you must commit to staying grounded and connected to your mission.

Manage your expectations.

Reality and expectations are two sides of the same coin; they are polarities. When you set an intention, you also create an expectation of what you want reality to become. If we don't dream, we can't make it real, and if we don't believe it, we can't expect it. It may sound like a paradox, but it is actually a cycle of polarities.

Expectations are about knowing where you are. Knowing your market, your strategies, and getting support. I believe that everybody needs support to grow; we all need someone to hold our hand along the way. Expectations are also about assessing and reviewing. If you're currently making $10,000 a month and you want to make $100,000, then there is a gap you need to cover. There is a process, a timeline from where you are to where you want to be. You need to find a method that works for you. There are no one-size-fits-all formulas.

It is easy to fall into the trap of instantaneous success and build expectations around it. Some marketers out there will tell you that they moved from five to, say, seven figures in three months. But they won't tell you the capacity and agency they had to build before those results came. The time, money, and support they needed to make that. Don't you ever compare your path to anybody else's! It is never about the numbers; it is about your energy and power. It is about building the proper foundations for growth. If you focus on your inner growth, results will inevitably come.

As you adjust your expectations to your particular situation, growth becomes fluid and natural, and you close those gaps more easily. There is nothing wrong with lowering your expectations to match your current capacity, but don't stay there. Stretch yourself a little bit more every day. When you get your first sale, you adjust. You gather evidence; you embody your power to both serve and receive. Then you level up. What comes next? And then next? All you need to do is start with a seed and move from there.

Avoid comparison because the first thing your ego will do is tell you that you can't get what others have achieved. Your ego wants to keep you safe, right where you are. It is avoiding change. Whenever you feel that inner, insecure voice inside you, ask yourself, *"What if I could get it? What would it feel like?"* Move out of judgment into inquiry and curiosity. With those come the reflection of where you currently are. Don't listen to anyone but yourself; listen to your intuition, your inner guidance. Therein lies the answer to what your next steps are. Trust it and move forward.

Soft is the new strong.

This phrase came up when I started practicing compassion, allowance, and acceptance. We are all aware of these concepts but don't know how to invite them into our lives. We don't have the skillset to embody compassion because our experiences are mainly based on judgment, and we're not even aware of that. These are inherited patterns, but we won't notice until we look deeply and honestly at what judgment feels like, and then ask ourselves what a life free of judgment also feels like. Judgment may not feel good, but it feels familiar. We're used to it. Is a human trait to judge ourselves.

Healthy judgment leads to a path of growth. We observe what needs to change and try to make it better. But when we stay in a judgment loop, just feeling bad about ourselves, it will disturb our energy and create illness. We get trapped in the victim mentality.

Judgment can lead to growth if it leads to compassion. They are both polarities. The framework for turning judgment into compassion is first noticing your judgmental patterns. It is not who you are; it is just a pattern you follow. Here in Australia, we tend to fall into the "don't-get-too-big-for-your-boots" narrative. "Who do you think you are?" as a societal pattern. So, must judgment come from outside of you. Notice the energies that come to play. Hold yourself grounded. Why is this showing up for you? Where is it coming from? Always be curious.

Often we feel judgment in our throat and our solar plexus. You may also feel anxious, have trouble sleeping, and begin to doubt yourself. You might even get sore feet because you can't move forward when you judge yourself. Pay attention to the nudges of pain or other sensations. If you're growing beyond the scope of what you know, as true warriors do, all the energetic patterns related to your place in society will activate. Especially your feet. They are a metaphor for the new steps you're taking and the new path you're creating.

There are a lot of things at play when we're in judgment. Judgment is not who you are, but it's in you, affecting you. It moves a lot of energy in the psycho-spiritual realms. So when you're experiencing all these sensations, ask yourself: *"Am I in judgment or in allowance and acceptance?"* Remember, judgment and compassion are polarities. You can move from one vibration to the opposite. Be kind to yourself and recognise you are here to make a difference. We all are.

Compassion starts with yourself. When you have compassion for yourself, you have direction and certainty. Accept and embrace that judgment will always be there as part of our narratives, but it's layered and multi-dimensional. Then move to compassion. It will give you a direction to follow and open your heart to receive more.

Keep up with your energetic practices.

Energetic hygiene means staying here on Earth. It's about grounding. It's never about protecting yourself within an energetic bubble but about connecting to your mission, increasing your vibration beyond your ego so that you never need protection again. I know dark forces. I've seen them and helped people overcome them. But if you are here and now, connected to your mission and vibrating at the frequency of joy, you will continue to stay grounded. Know yourself enough not to let external influences distract you.

Do your daily energetic and spiritual work. I'm committed to daily thirty-minute meditation, or sometimes even more. I keep an eye on my stress levels and take note of my nuances and the changes in my body. I rest when I'm overwhelmed.

Get your feet on the grass or the ground to do your grounding. Feel your feet. Most of us sit with our feet up or one foot up. When we're sitting on a chair, especially in the office chair, most women sit with their foot behind the other foot. Try to keep both your feet solidly on the ground. Go barefoot as much as possible because that connection to Earth is always good.

Use astrology as a tool to know yourself.

When I first knew about astrology as a tool, it was like finding a missing link. Because my chart doesn't have a lot of Earth signs, I have trouble grounding myself. I had to work hard to be grounded. I have a hard time with human, worldly things. I get stressed and overwhelmed easily. But that has an upside because, as an intuitive, it's easy for me to tap into the realms of the unseen.

Knowing about myself on that level made me understand so many things! It was the missing link I needed. That is why I recommend you do your research and get to know your astrology chart. There are many sites where you can get them for free. You should at least know your Sun Sign, Ascendant/Rising sign and Moon Sign. There are many layers to explore here. Your birth chart is a rich dialogue between what you know, who you are, and the external influences that can play havoc. I highly recommend getting to know at least the basics of your natal astrology chart. It is steeped in gold nuggets.

Many of the misunderstandings we experience with others come from our different signs. For example, a fire sign has trouble understanding a sensitive Pisces, a water sign. Some of my clients have triple fire, air, earth, or water signs. That requires some attention on their part on how to balance their energy and how to connect with others. Look for the signs –

it really helps to accept you and your elemental energy style and nuance. This may be your case as well.

Astrology can be predictive, but most of all, it gives you an understanding of the layers in you. It can also help you assess the Moon cycles and how they affect you. The Moon affects tides, creates typhoons, and has a powerful effect on water. Humans are made 70% out of water; don't you think it can affect us too? We gravitate towards the Moon's energy. I constantly feel the Moon and its influence and how it affects my energy level. Give it a try yourself. Be curious!

Chapter 12 - The Magical Warrior

*A*ll the inner work we've done culminates here. These tools will help you manifest your intentions, stay grounded, and follow your soul's purpose. Use them whenever things get a bit shaky, when you feel your energy shift, when you are going through an energetic upgrade, or just to get curious and gather evidence.

Just have fun with them! They work!

I first came to know these tools when I was around twenty. I booked a holiday in Fiji for my husband Mark and myself. We still had no children, but we were already married. Mark has always been the grounding voice, and he was wondering how we would make it happen. I told him not to worry, with absolute certainty that it would happen. He was skeptical and asked what was going to happen and how. We didn't have any money. But then, even in my twenties, I didn't know how or when, but I told him, *"don't worry, it'll happen."* That is just who I am. Then one day, I found a bank book I'd forgotten, with over $700 in spending money. Was that a coincidence? Maybe, but would I have found it if I didn't need the money? I think it's magic. I believe with my whole being, magic is real. We had our spending money. It was a lot back then.

Years later, I wanted to go to New York. I was running and training with a personal trainer. I wanted to combine my running with a business trip; I thought I could do a bit of branding and business support and run the New York Marathon. So, I rang an agent because I knew it was hard to get into the New York Marathon without one. That year they had 40 spots for Australia and just one left. I got it. Another time I attended a conference in Australia. One of the conference leaders was teaching a course in Seattle the next month. I decided to attend even if I wasn't sure where the money would come from. I just felt a strong pull to it. That course led me to the trajectory of my soul's mission. I manifested by just saying yes to my intuition.

These things happen quite regularly. Magic happens all the time. That is why I believe the saying, *"be careful what you wish for because you may get it,"* it's true. All you need to do is wish. The Universe delivers when you ask and take consistent action. Even if that action means lighting a candle and believing that the next step will be revealed at the right time. Never fall into that cave where you stop believing your wishes are possible.

Make a wish.

One day my sister asked me about wishes after a 12-12 event I held online. She said: *"Maria, how do I make a wish? Is there a right way to ask?"* Whenever you ask for a wish or do a spell, it should hold an intention made with a visceral connection. It must be embodied in a way that gives you chills or feels a bit scary. Let that conviction of it coming true transpire. Then, let go of control. You can't control a thing. A wish rarely comes the way you think it will.

A typical block to making wishes are religious narratives. We inherit those from our lineage, with many layers to them. In essence, become the joyful child you were meant to be, and bring her spirit out to play. You will find that the world is really magical.

I met with my cousin at my mother's house one day. She has a young daughter who, at the time, was four or five. We were making traditional Christmas cakes. We sprinkled fairy dust over the cakes, and it felt so magical! We cast a spell, so when people eat it, they would feel the love that was put into them. After we said the spell, we clapped three times. Doing magic isn't hard. I genuinely believe it's a simple process. The cakes were divinely delicious. Was that the work of magic? Maybe, or maybe not. You decide. But there is something special in the magic we put into everything we do.

I've worked with people that held all kinds of intentions. Some wanted to find love, others wanted to have children and get pregnant, and others wanted more clients or money. I've worked with people who want to improve their health. It's all the same. All we do is ask for it and then do the spiritual work to pave the way for your wish to come through.

Cast a spell.

When we make a wish, we create a reality ahead of time. We envision it, and it becomes visceral. This means you imagine how it would feel if your desire manifests; you sensationalise it. Now you are in the process of self-actualisation, an intimate awareness of self. As you feel your wish enter your reality, even if it's still in your mind, you are actualising, which becomes a prophecy. It is as if your wish has come true. It's a quantum transformation.

Your wishes are in the ethers. When you cast a spell, you say them out loud, for example, three times. Use language but also use your feelings. Casting a spell is a signal to the Universe that we are ready to receive what we want. It's a conscious invitation for the wish to come true.

You will experience some resistance. All your subconscious stories will come up, giving you reasons why you can't have what you wish for. Become aware of what comes after casting a spell because if you don't believe, it won't come true. Taking action is even easier than believing. The ego has a strong impulse to keep us safe where we are. I share this with you after going through my own transformation process and witnessing lots of transformation in people. That messy part in the middle is the gold. If we stay there, question our stories, and let go of our resistance, we will surely get our wishes.

Universal frequencies have accelerated, so our ability to manifest and actualise has also increased. This has been happening progressively over the past ten years due to our ability to access information, connection and the world wide net – the Internet. If you are inspired to take action and follow the steps to manifest your wishes, this is a great time to do so.

The manifestation process requires you to be fully present. When you have a dream, you're projecting yourself into a future event, which can confuse many people. How can we be present and focus on what is yet to come? Your wish is in your heart. You can see it, feel it, you *are* it. You are bringing your wish forward into the present moment.

There's no linear time. It's an illusion. Just trust the Universe will bring what you need at the right moment. It is not always exactly the way you envision it. You don't know what the best way is, so trust. Come back to your heart and believe. Is it true for you? If not, then it won't happen. If it's true for you, then it will.

Be curious about what is coming. Doesn't matter the language, the ritual, or the spell you used, all that matters is your energy. Are you opening the space for your wish to manifest? Manifesting is a skill set that comes with practice. And with it also comes maturity and experience.

Bend time.

Another part of the quantum work we do as warriors is bending timelines. Time isn't set in stone, even if we believe it is. Time is a mental construct. As humans, we feel constantly pressured. So, first, you must recognise the stress around you. Then do an energy audit, including what's going on astrologically. Those energy audits can uncover many levels for you. You might discover you are responding to energies that don't belong to you or have been imposed on you. You might find that the Moon or other cosmic energies such as the planets affect your mood and perception of time, making you experience pressure. We are all gravitational beings.

Bending time means adjusting our perception of how much time we have. It's part of the abundance mindset. The best practice I use for bending time is slowing down. I know this sounds counterintuitive, but when you feel the pressure of not having enough time, go back to your breath, move into that space where time is just an illusion, and let your intuition guide you.

What can you prioritise?
What can you do with that?

Let all the external pressures go and just flow with your intuition. You'll see how much you can get done in such little time. You might also find that tasks in your to-do list solved themselves without your intervention. It's true magic!

Here is a ritual I use to bend time. On the first of the month, I set up a time clock made up of 12 one-dollar coins. I placed the coins in a clock formation. In the middle, I put a candle, previously dressed and programmed. To program the candle, I whisper sweet intentions to it. So that every time I light it, it lights my path. Reminds me of my intention. And I'm working with an ally, the Goddess of Fortuna, who supports my intention too. This is a ritual I share with my clients, and we are working together to time-bend so that time is our ally and supports us to achieve what we desire.

Test and measure.

Your muscle fibers grow when you break them down. They need to stretch a little, hurt a little, and re-build in a new, more oversized shape. The same thing happens when you want to grow. You need to expand a little more with each new goal. You must stretch your comfort zone each time to the point that it feels scary.

As you go through new experiences and make decisions, sometimes things will go as planned, and sometimes they won't. Sometimes you'll be happy with the results, and others, you won't like it. Forget about the narrative of making mistakes. Treat it all as a test. There is no failing involved in this process. You are simply trying something new to see what happens; you're engaging with life from a sense of curiosity.

As you move forward, ask yourself:

Does this feel good for me?

This will be your first approach to measuring your results. So, you test something, then measure; test and measure; test and measure. It's an ongoing process. You can use qualitative or quantitative systems to measure your results; it doesn't matter, as long as you are always deeply connected to your soul. Always ask if any decision or course of action feels in alignment with you. If it just feels *right* to you.

Use magical props and rituals.

There's a school of thought that says you don't need anything external to yourself to manifest, that it's all about mind and vibration. As much as I believe in the Law of Correspondence – as within, so without –– I also believe in the physicality of our human experience. We need to embody our intentions, to fully sensationalise them. Rituals and magical props are great tools to do so. Plus, it's easier for the mind to grasp something external, an actual tangible experience than to work only with the intangible and ethereal.

Magic is inherently in you. It's in all of us. So, play with tools and props. I love Mother Nature tools. I play with flowers, herbs, or crystals, but there is a wide variety of tools, so here are some ideas for you to get started:

Lighting a candle.

This is probably the easiest one because we all have a candle at home. Does it have to be a specific size, shape, or color depending on your intention? It could, but don't overcomplicate it. I always tell my clients that if they don't have the time to do more complex rituals, simply light a candle to Source, your guides, or your intention. It's super simple, so no excuses. Just light the effin' candle!

Sacred Geometry.

The Universe is created in perfect mathematical order, and its language is geometry. Ancient sages like Aristotle, Plato, the Egyptians, and Hermetics used sacred geometry to understand and access the secret powers of the Universe. Sacred geometry is the hidden mathematical language of nature. It can be found everywhere, from the tiniest grain of sand to the shapes of galaxies. It's the magical, perfect order of the Universe binding everything together. Geometrical representations of these shapes and divine proportions are venerated in many ancient cultures. The most common figures are the Flower of Life, the Merkaba, known as Metatron's Cube, and the Golden Spiral. You can use some of these shapes to meditate on your intention or write it on a piece of paper with sacred geometry drawn on it.

Crystals and crystal grids.

Some of my favourite magic tools are crystals and crystal grids. Crystal grids are an arrangement of crystals in a sacred geometry shape that we charge with a clear intention. Crystals hold in their structure the essence of that Sacred Geometry. They are powerful because they bring pieces of the world together: location, energy, and lifetimes of connection.

Sigils and symbols.

Numbers and words have energy; they are alive. They have a frequency that holds power to attract what you want. You can look for symbols or symbolic numbers, such as Angel Numbers or Grabovoi codes. Simply look for the magic number for your intention and recite it or repeat it in your head. Then say thank you for your intentions are in the way of manifesting. To create a sigil, write your intention on a piece of paper, using as few letters as possible. For example, instead of *"I want more money,"* simply write *"money."* Then remove the vowels from the word. You'll be left with *"mny."* Draw all letters together in a unique shape, or simply draw them on top of each other. Don't judge the process; it's supposed to be fun, not perfectly beautiful. Once it's done, place your sigil strategically in your office or bedroom to help you manifest.

Card decks.

Cards are a great instrument to get guidance. There are several out in the market, and you can purchase them for little. To use your deck, ask your spirit guides an open question. This can be *"What do I need to know to..."* or *"How can I...?"* Don't ask yes-no questions. Shuffle the card and pick one from the deck. You'll be surprised by what will come out!

Sacred adornments.

Jewellery as a talisman, and amulets also have a powerful vibration. Crystal necklaces, rings, or bracelets are very powerful. Wear them! Even religious or pagan medallions will work. They are beautiful, and remember that you are the one who gives meaning and an intention to them.

Plants and essential oils.

I love plants and all-natural elements. They are perfect for stimulating your senses and raising your vibration. I use sage and Palo Santo for energy clearing. You can use them for manifesting, amplifying and magnifying energy, relaxation, energising, or even as medicine for illness. Herbs and essential oils are potent too. The right combination can create magic beyond your dreams.

Invocation and prayer.

This one is as basic as lighting a candle, but we tend to forget its power. Praying is nothing but openly asking the Divine for whatever you want or need; it's a support request. Don't be afraid to ask! An invocation is calling on spirits and guides with intention. It's crucial to sensationalise your invocation.

New Moon Ritual.

I already explained why working with the Moon can be so powerful. We work with the moon phases in agriculture. It's the same for business and other intentions. The ancients knew what the New Moon represented; it's about new beginnings and planting the seeds to cultivate and harvest in time. We should always plant seeds during a New Moon phase because it's when they can go deep into darkness and get nurtured by the soil and the water. Make your New Moon wishes. Make your wish and burn it outside, or bury it deep in the soil. Make three to eight wishes at each New Moon.

Full Moon Ritual

The Full Moon illuminates our shadow elements, those things we don't like about ourselves, all the things we want to release. That is why everything is heightened at the Full Moon; it's illumination on all levels. This is a powerful Full Moon Release ritual: take a Bay Leaf, write on both sides using a black permanent marker *"release,"* and then *"fear and doubt"* on the flip side; then burn it. It will burn quickly if you are ready to release it all. If you doubt your ability to release it, it will burn slowly. You might even have to relight it. Work with it. This labour will help you commit, and then it releases with ease. It's a Universal Soul Message.

Join a circle.

It's easier to manifest anything you desire if you get support. We tend to overthink and doubt ourselves and our powers. Magic happens when we see others achieve what we want or even struggle with the same issues we do. We gather evidence and build knowledge as a collective, making us feel more secure and helping us accelerate our learning process. Our reality expands, and we embody what's possible beyond our limited experience.

We set an intention each month in my Women's Circle. Each intention is tried and tested. We work with crystals. We share our individual intentions. This all happens online; each member is at home. Still, given that we are all using the same elements and principles, and we are programming our grids simultaneously, we are building energetic momentum. We are regular women, performing the magic inherent to every human being. We are holding hands energetically; we are striving to be of service to the community for the greater good. We're doing the work together.

Every week several members manifest their intentions. I get lots of *"Maria! This works! I can't believe it!"* Of course, it does! If you've ever been in a prayer circle or a meditation group, you know the power of all intentions and energies coming together. My experience both with myself and my clients is that this work helps. That is why I keep a journal to document and gather the evidence. I recommend you do the same. Do a magic journal and track your results.

Start with the simple work of lighting a candle, and see what happens. I've seen people heal and manifest all sorts of wishes. They tell me they feel more relaxed and in control and experience less fear. These rituals really work!

If you want to learn more about my Circles, visit my website, I'll be thrilled to have you!

Conclusion.

Congratulations to you, brave, magical, manifesting Warrior! I have just one final message for you: **don't hide!**

Don't hide your gifts. Don't hide them from yourself. Don't hide them from those who you're here to serve.

Don't hide the fact that you don't know. Maybe you need more information on creating money or getting fair compensation for what you do. Know that you're supported if you step up to your platform and truly provide your gifts as a service to create a better world.

I know that sounds really big. There's something extraordinary and magical on a soul level for you. Being the worrier helps you fit in. Being a Warrior enables you to stand out and meet your soul's commitment.

> *Things are easy. Things are not hard.*
> *Just look at the evidence. It's all there.*
> *Magic is real, and it's in you.*

Thank you for holding the space to become your best.

Love, Maria.

Acknowledgements

I want to thank my teachers and students along the way. Standing in the playground after my youngest went to school, speaking passionately about me going back to school. From this my first business was born. My first client hired me before I'd even qualified as a Personal Trainer. That was the beginning of my entrepreneurship journey. I built up quite a following in my local community. To this day, people ask "when are we going back to your fitness classes. I loved them".

My Running Coach who saw potential in me. Pulled the strength and resilience up. Supported me to muster the courage to take the steps in training and complete the steps in the marathons.

My anatomy teacher who introduced me to the concept of spirituality and body. There is nothing like being in a wet lab going through the layers both physically and metaphorically. Witnessing the issues in the tissues in real matter. Matter matters. He was a theologian too. It was life changing.

Grateful to Rosie, who gave her body to science. Rosie was the owner of body lying there in the wet lab ready to teach and show me so many things about the layers. She also taught me about Clairvoyance and Claireaudience. When she started to speak to me and share her stories. I thought I was crazy for the longest times but she helped me see that I had a gift to share to support others to heal.

My Kinesiologist who helped me see the unseen but deeply felt. Introducing me to the language of medical intuition. Up till then I thought my sensitivity was a curse. But my sensitivity and knowing had proven to be a gift to support me and others to know and access healing within.

My first Circle sister who said - Maria hold a Circle, pick a date and offer to women. You can do it! Seven years later I am still holding space for women to acknowledge and reclaim their brilliance in the world.

My deep gratitude to all those who supported me along me own cancer journey. It cemented that whatever you send out into the world, you receive back ten fold. I sent out a lot of healing and I received it all back. Healing from cancer was a big journey which felt supported and sacred. Learnings and shifts were huge.

Holding space for my future Circle soul sisters, I welcome you into the unseen yet deeply felt world of energy, matrix and void. May you reclaim your wisdom and strength to be the leader you are. The work continues as we heal seven generations back and seven generations forward. The legacy is to leave the world a better world, a healed world. It begins with the one and ends in the collective. We truly are all one.

Resources

As you have read throughout the book, there are specific videos, blog posts, and webinars with all the basics that will allow you to continue your journey from Worrier to Warrior. **Visit:** www.mariaheals.com/worrier-to-warrior

For more working with Astrology.

- The big 3 in your astrological chart: Sun Sign, Ascendent and Moon
- The Moon & You

For more on crystals...

- Crystals for Business Success
- Everything You Need to Know About Crystal Grids

For more on soul-aligned business strategies...

- Soul-Powered Launch Hacks
- Business Leadership & Magic

To get you started with rituals and spells...

- 5 Days - 5 Spells

Printed in Great Britain
by Amazon